Celebration of Sisters

It Is Never Too Late To Grieve

JUDY LIPSON

North Carolina

Published in the United States by WriteLife Publishing
(an imprint of Boutique of Quality Books Publishing Company, Inc.)
www.writelife.com

978-1-60808-267-4 (p)
978-1-60808-268-1 (e)

Library of Congress Control Number: 2021947051

Book Design by Robin Krauss, www.bookformatters.com
Cover Design by Rebecca Lown, www.rebeccalowndesign.com
Cover concept by BiancoMarchilonis Design,
  www.biancomarchilonis.com
Photography/Art Direction by Peter Bianco
First editor: Allison Itterly
Second editor: Andrea Vande Vorde

Praise for
Celebration of Sisters
and Judy Lipson

"With her memoir *Celebration of Sisters*, Judy Lipson breaks her family's traditional code of silence by sharing her story —stark, candid, and impassioned: a love letter to her sisters. By describing her role as the middle sister in a sister trio, and remembering the lives and premature deaths of both of her sisters—one to a car accident, and the other to a chronic eating disorder—Judy bravely faces these great losses, and in turn, moves through her grief. Told through vivid memories from early childhood through adulthood, the arc of Judy's story engages the reader with its intimacy. The message, that talking openly about loss and mental health is healing, will resound with readers from all walks of life.

– Kamryn T. Eddy, Ph.D and Jennifer J. Thomas, Ph.D
Co-Directors, Eating Disorders Clinical and Research Program, Massachusetts General Hospital Associate Professors, Department of Psychiatry, Harvard Medical School

"Author Judy Lipson shares with her readers beautiful, poignant family memories that bring tears and smiles and ultimately presents a story of survival and yearning for better days. Judy's book will touch your heart from beginning to end and inspire with the simple message, out of loss and despair there is hope."

– Joanne Vassallo Jamrosz,
author of the *Skating Forward* series

"Judy's story is so moving, from the time she was a young woman up until now, building such strength through family tragedy. So inspiring!"

– Randy Gardner, Two-time Olympian,
U.S. World Pair Champion

To my sisters, Margie and Jane. I will always love you.

Table of Contents

Introduction

When I lost my twenty-two-year-old sister Jane in a tragic automobile accident in 1981, and then my thirty-five-year-old sister Margie after a twenty-year battle with anorexia and bulimia in 1990, my life changed forever. Unable to believe in the reality of my losses, I shut down for years that turned into decades. After thirty years of keeping my grief dormant, confronting my feelings was not an easy journey. As an intensely private person, divulging my inner soul to others—a necessary step in facing my heartbreak—required me to step far outside my comfort zone. But this was a mission I needed to accomplish for myself and my sisters, and one that I hope will help others. It wasn't until I could finally grieve that I felt I had brought Margie and Jane home, and subsequently, all of us to a place of comfort.

Why did I fight to confront my grief now after thirty years of silence? Signs appeared. In 2010, I ran into one of Jane's friends, and then one of Margie's friends. Both wanted to talk to me about my sisters, and I just stood there unable to speak. My father was diagnosed with a terminal illness and passed away in 2011, another tremendous loss. My best friend was diagnosed with terminal cancer. Waves of grief churned around me, but I could no longer ignore them.

When my sisters passed away, I not only lost them, but I

also lost many of our stories. All I have left are the fragments of my own memory—a memory that was altered because of my inability to grieve after each sister's death and the trauma of Margie's long illness. Even so, I felt sure that the love of my sisters would carry me through the writing of this book, and I am grateful that it did.

In Judaism, it is common to give and receive gifts in multiples of eighteen dollars or *chai*, meaning "life" and "giving back." I chose to structure this book into eighteen sections in the hope that it will offer something back to its readers. After years of denial, I finally gave myself permission to take care of myself and find a way to hold my grief with grace. If, in telling my story, one person feels less alone, I will be eternally grateful. *Celebration of Sisters* is my journey in sharing my story and my sisters with you.

PROLOGUE

I Will Always Love You

MEMORY: JANE SAT ON THE SOFA. MARGIE SANG "HAPPI-
NESS" FROM THE SHOW YOU'RE A GOOD MAN, CHARLIE
BROWN. I SAT ON THE PIANO BENCH PLAYING ALONG. "HAP-
PINESS IS HAVING A SISTER . . ."

The premiere of the Celebration of Sisters ice-skating event was
about to start, and Whitney Houston's "I Will Always Love
You" filled the arena. At fifty-six years old, I was about to skate
in my first ice dancing performance in a duet with my coach. I
wore a purple dress, my favorite color, and black trunks from
my youth as a skater, surprised they fit after all these years,
over beige tights. I floated across the ice with my partner,
skating faster, and crossed one foot over the other to gain
momentum, then jumped up onto my partner's knee, my arm
outstretched to the sky. His arm encircled my waist, providing
me with added security. The crowd embraced our enthusiasm
with applause and cheers. My exhilarating ice dance was a
triumphant declaration. *Look at me! I did it!*

As my partner eased me down and spun me around for our
final pose to thunderous applause, I felt my chest thunder, and I
smiled from ear to ear. I could not help recalling the small Belle
Isle Rink where it all started. It was the first place where I'd
ice-skated with my sisters, Margie and Jane. On the day of our
first group lesson, we'd felt so proud to carry our new white
Riedell skates into the rink. Margie, the natural athlete, took to

ice-skating immediately. I struggled and putted along. Jane had been somewhere in the middle.

Ice-skating brought me full circle back to my beloved sisters. As I glided across the ice, I felt free and the weight of my world lifted. I imagined Margie and Jane skating on each side of me, holding onto my shoulders. The joy at my sisters' presence reflected in my radiant face and fluid movements on the ice. I was able to dance away from the pain for that one moment in time. Ice-skating was and is my passion, solace, and peace.

Margie and Jane, I will always love you.

CHAPTER 1

Jane

MEMORY: "I'M DRIVING!" "NO, I'M DRIVING!" OF COURSE, BEING THE OLDER SISTER ON OUR LAST SHOPPING OUTING TOGETHER ON COMMONWEALTH AVENUE, I WON OUT. JANE RODE SHOTGUN AS I LAUGHED—AND SHE LAUGHED, TOO, REVEALING THE DIMPLE IN HER RIGHT CHEEK.

On Saturday morning, November 7, 1981, my phone jolted me awake. My phone never rang at eight thirty, especially on Saturdays when I tended to sleep in. I'd had a fitful night's sleep, as that had been my first night in my New York City apartment. I bolted upright in bed, taking a moment to focus on where I was.

A job promotion had brought me back to New York after a brief stint in Washington, DC. My new position as branch coordinator for Bloomingdale's eleven luxury department stores required me to travel to Massachusetts, New York, New Jersey, and Pennsylvania to ensure consistency in service and practices. I was also the liaison between the different branches and the central buying office.

I loved my new studio apartment in Union Square, off Fifth Avenue, with its good-sized galley kitchen and separate dressing area. Three weeks earlier, I'd strolled down city streets feeling triumphant. I had received a promotion from Bloomingdale's. *I am twenty-five years old and living in New York City,* I thought. *My life is great.*

Of course, my mother, Ellie, didn't love the location of my apartment. When she came to help on moving day, she practically told the moving men to turn the truck around. But then she saw the twenty-four-hour doorman for the building and was satisfied. She helped me unpack and settle in, then returned home to Boston for my younger sister's twenty-second birthday. My mother was taking Jane to see *Dreamgirls.*

"Judy, did I wake you?" my aunt Stel said over the phone.

I yawned. "Yeah . . . sort of."

"Listen, I have some shoes that I want to drop off," she said. This was not unusual. My aunt had a career in the shoe business, and for years had provided me with shoes. Lucky for me that my foot was the sample size.

Less than ten minutes later, my aunt and cousin showed up and were pacing around my apartment. Although my aunt presented a cool demeanor to others, she and I shared a special closeness. We both lived in New York, worked in retail, and liked to crochet. My studio apartment housed a small sofa where the two finally sat as I opened the bags of shoes my aunt had brought. There was a pair of brown Amalfi shoes with a low heel and a navy pair with a sling back.

Suddenly, the phone rang. It was my parents. They had bad news. In that moment, my world changed in an instant.

My heart stopped. I immediately thought of my older sister, Margie, who had been sick. How many times had my sister been on the verge of death? But it was my adorable younger sister, Jane, who was gone. I cannot remember their exact words. Whatever they were, I didn't believe them. Jane had died instantly in a tragic automobile accident. *Why?* I remember thinking. *What does this mean?* She had just celebrated her twenty-second birthday the day before.

My parents had called my aunt so I would not be alone to receive the horrific news. Margie was already en route to New York City to celebrate her own birthday with me the next day. She didn't know yet. She would be at my apartment in a few hours. A sick feeling settled in my stomach. I would have to tell her that our sister Jane had died.

While we waited for Margie, my aunt helped me pack to go home. I was clueless as I walked around my new studio apartment. My efficient mother helped me unpack and settle in. Everything unpacked, put away, pictures hung on the wall. Having lived in a hotel for a month while my apartment was getting ready, I was still getting used to where my belongings were. Where were my clothes, my suitcase, my travel toiletries? I couldn't locate anything and was floundering around. I was usually so organized, but I could not focus. I was grateful my aunt and my cousin were there to help navigate the packing process and travel logistics.

I didn't know how long I would be gone. My cobalt-blue suitcase with the gold strap down the middle somehow got packed, half empty, with whatever black clothing I owned.

Then there was a knock on the door. Margie arrived.

Knowing I had to divulge the news frightened me. I opened the door and was shocked by my older sister's appearance. She looked like a lost child. Her small statue seemed even tinier, cheekbones more pronounced, coat falling off her shoulders, and the overnight bag overpowered her. But Margie knew immediately that something was terribly wrong. She just stood in the doorway and did not move.

"We lost Jane," I blurted. That was one of the hardest moments in my life.

My aunt somehow managed to get us both back into the apartment. The focus naturally had to be on Margie. We both were hysterical. My aunt and cousin calmed us down and scurried around making arrangements so we could fly home to Boston. Or perhaps the arrangements had already been made by my parents. I have no memory.

At some point I called my best friend, Denise. She and her boyfriend came over. They were both speechless. The hugs were greatly appreciated. I could see the pain in Denise's eyes. A vision of Jane and me in my car flashed through my mind. At the end of Jane's freshman year at CW Post on Long Island, I had driven down from Boston to pick her up. I remembered how good that trip was. Jane hadn't treated me as an outcast, which felt good for a change, though I think my status might have been elevated because Jane herself was at such a low point. Her freshman year had not been successful. I'd stayed overnight. The next day, we'd loaded up my father's green Buick and drove home without any major fights despite our close quarters.

I couldn't believe Jane was gone.

I gave Denise a key to my apartment, and she promised to take care of things for me in New York. I didn't know how long I would be gone from my new home.

The one-hour flight from New York to Boston seemed like an eternity. Margie and I held hands and cried for the entire flight. Family friends picked us up at the airport. Inside our childhood home, people were scattered around the house in silence. It was all a blur. My father grabbed Margie and me and embraced us in hugs. My mother was curled in a chair, her body racked with irrepressible sobs. Margie and I went to her.

That evening, I tossed and turned in bed. In the wee hours of the morning, I finally succumbed to a fitful sleep but was awakened by a terrible dream. Startled, frightened, and disoriented in my adolescent, pitch-dark bedroom, I felt relieved to see my mother. She couldn't sleep either, so she had come into my room and turned on the light. We cried together.

On Sunday, November 8, Margie's birthday, people streamed in and out of the house offering their condolences, but it was all a blur. Margie and I sat in my father's study trying to put together our thoughts about our sister Jane on orange-lined paper. We just couldn't bring ourselves out into the fray of people and chatter.

The funeral was held on Monday at Stanetsky's Funeral Home. I suppose there was a large gathering, but I don't remember much of it.

The rabbi read our words as part of his eulogy.

Jane—to us always, Janie—our dear, sweet little sister, you were the essence of this sisterhood to us. From our earliest memories on Indian Ridge Road, when you cried having your picture taken—you were always so cute, lovable, and at times trying, but always, our dream sister. We walked you to school, we fought with you, we protected you from dogs, we ate Raisinets together on Saturday nights. We grew up together through thick and thin—all the good and the bad. But most of all, we loved each other. Words are not enough. We just want to say, we will always love you.

I have no recollection of Jane's funeral. Immediately after, our family began the Jewish tradition of sitting shiva, when the family stays home to grieve, remember their loved one, and receive visitors. My sole memory of the shiva week was with my mother's friend Audrey. People brought lots of food, and the kitchen counters were loaded with platters of bagels, lox, cream cheese, deli meats, cookies and pastries, and fruits. I never understood the need for so much food. I supposed it was more for the visitors, not the immediate family. None of us could eat.

I will never forget what Audrey said that day when she pulled me aside. "There will come a time when you won't remember your sister," she said softly. Her words stayed with me for three decades. I often felt tortured because I could not remember everything about my sisters after they passed away.

The week after Jane died, I was still in a complete fog, unable to believe my sister was gone. Yet, I was whisked back to my life in New York City. I think my father wanted me to resume my "normal" life and separate me from my mother, whose grief left her hanging by a thread.

I was thrust into the height of the Christmas season for the retail industry. Yearly sales depended on this condensed period. Whatever your position in the company, "all hands on deck" was the motto, which meant everyone had to be on the sales floor helping customers at all times. My cousin, who also worked at Bloomingdale's, had notified Human Resources that my sister's death was the reason for my week-long absence.

On my first day back to work after Jane's passing, my body shook and I started weeping. I could not hold it together. The familiar door, desks, chairs, and hallways seemed foreign, out of place. A very kind coworker escorted me into his office where I sat and cried. I had always been so strong and had held everything and everyone together. I *had* to compose myself. I worked for a tyrant of a boss who had no tolerance for crying and no compassion for what I was going through. Had I cried in front of her, my career in retail would have been finished.

Over the next few weeks, I walked through the motions of

my life like a robot in a fog. Often, my concentration floated away. At times, customer demands seemed so frivolous. I had no choice but to smile and provide excellent customer service in an attempt to hold onto my reputation as always providing a stellar job performance. So I just kept moving. No time to think about the fact that I recently buried my younger sister. I did not understand grief, the process, or the experience. There was no one to talk to. I had no clue what I felt. On the outside, no one knew I'd lost my sister. I did not talk about it with anyone, and if anyone did know, they did not bring it up to me. The glow in my personality that people used to comment on had evaporated. My being felt empty.

Thanksgiving had always been my favorite holiday. I always traveled home. I loved the smell of the turkey cooking in the oven and watching the Macy's Thanksgiving Day Parade on television with my sisters. That year, dinner invitations had arrived from assorted family and friends. It was only three weeks after Jane's death, so our family decided to have Thanksgiving dinner in a restaurant. Margie was not present—I don't remember why—so my parents and I sat at the table in the restaurant and picked at our food. The evening was devoid of laughter and conversation. We each held empty space in our hearts to contain Jane's absence . . . and Margie's.

That Thanksgiving weekend, my closest friend from high school got married. I was a bridesmaid and did not want to disappoint her. I was suddenly living by a code of silence and secrets about my grief, and I never expressed my feelings to my friend, so I put up a good front and showed up for her.

Dressed in a burgundy bridesmaid's dress, my legs shook and my knees kept buckling as I walked down the aisle. No one there knew that I had recently lost my sister. While dancing with one of the groomsmen, I blurted out that my sister had died three weeks ago. We stopped dancing and he stared at me. Then I proceeded through the movements of the wedding celebration. When I look back on it, I don't know how I had the strength. I was still in shock over Jane's death.

December was cold and lonely. New York City was decorated with lights and Christmas music played on every station. There was joy in the air, but my heart was broken. I loved window-shopping with friends during the holidays, ice-skating at Rockefeller Center, having a hot chocolate at Serendipity . . . but it all passed that season.

After Jane's death, Margie and I, working long retail hours, did not communicate very often. Although we did not speak about our loss, Margie sent me a poem she'd written. She expressed her feelings so eloquently in her own words.

Who has broken into our lives?
Who has spoken to our brokenness?
Who keeps breaking into our presence?
We don't have all the answers.
We do have a lot of questions.
We search in a world of bereft.
Descend upon our hearts, for we need renewing away.
We await your love and power to heal and bless.
Refresh us now. Enlighten us now.
Our bodies have given us pain and we need healing.
Our emotions have been bruised, and we need your comfort.
Descend upon our hearts this day.

Looking back, I realize how much I had changed and how much my family had changed with that one phone call. A part of all of us was gone and could never be replaced. I did not know who I was. We had always been three sisters. Now we were two.

CHAPTER 2

Margie

MEMORY: IN THE CROWDED SYNAGOGUE, JANE, AGE FIVE, STOOD UP, WAVED HER ARMS, AND YELLED, "HI, MARGIE!" AS MARGIE CROSSED THE BIMAH AT TEMPLE TO RECEIVE HER CERTIFICATE OF CONSECRATION FROM HEBREW SCHOOL.

When I opened the door on August 1, 1990, and saw my parents standing in the hallway outside of my apartment, I immediately *knew*. Just a few days earlier, my father and I talked over coffee. "Judy, we are going to lose her this time," he'd said. Now, no words needed to be spoken. The inevitable had come. My older sister Margie had lost her years-long battle with anorexia and bulimia. My beloved Margie was gone. That Wednesday evening in August is forever etched in my mind.

My parents entered my apartment. They hugged my two young daughters, ages three and five, who jumped up and down. "Hi, Grandma and Papa, come see our drawings!" Janie and Amy shouted. Somehow, I held back my tears until my parents left.

I sat my daughters down and said, "Mommy is very sad that Auntie Margie died." I cried and my daughters, one on each side, hugged me. They did not understand loss but knew something was amiss.

Later, I flung myself onto my bed and sobbed. Dutifully, I

made a few phone calls. I repeated the same story to all: "I have sad news, my sister Margie died." After they expressed their condolences, I abruptly ended the call and moved on to the next one. Most of my newer friends I met after college did not know Margie. Unable to express or comprehend the magnitude of loss, I revealed little to others. How could they share in the enormity of my pain or the dreadful impact Margie's death had on me?

Exhausted from the phone calls and news of Margie's death, sleep did not come. My daughters needed me. *And what about my parents?* So I put up a strong front and raced forward. A deep, lonely anguish overwhelmed me.

The day after Margie's death, I became fidgety. Margie died on a Wednesday, her funeral would be on a Friday, and the waiting around made me restless. People gathered at my parents' home. My daughters provided distraction to the family and friends who were scattered throughout the living room and kitchen. But the forced small talk and awkwardness of others not knowing what to say exhausted me. Along with my closest friends, I retired to the small den. When the small talk got under my skin, I shut it down.

I called a friend and asked her to bring over a needlepoint. She wanted to know what design. "Anything," I said. "I just need to keep my hands busy and block out the chatter." Within a short time, she arrived. I completed the parrot design in record time, my hands moving fast to distract me.

I did not own anything black to wear to Margie's funeral, so a close family friend took me shopping to buy a black skirt. The break from the nonsense chatter at my parents' home felt good. In the midst of the scorching August heat and funeral arrangements, we went to Hit or Miss in Newton Center. I did not care about the skirt, but during that hour of shopping, the people who helped me were kind and compassionate; they *really* looked at me and they recognized my loss.

Margie's funeral was held in our temple, not in a funeral home, probably because Margie had kept in touch with the rabbi on a regular basis. The family sequestered in the Bride's Room adjacent to the back entrance of the large sanctuary that had gorgeous stained-glass windows. To walk to the ladies' room required walking down a long hall through the main lobby where several people started trickling in for the service. Not wanting to engage in conversation with anyone, I scooted quickly to the ladies' room.

My mother was standing at the sink blowing her nose and putting on lipstick. My closest friend, whom I spoke with every day, followed me in. She had never met Margie or Jane, but she felt my pain, and she started crying. Then I burst into tears. We wrapped our arms around each other in a big hug.

"Stop crying," my mother snapped. My friend and I stared at each other in disbelief, frozen, unsure what to do.

I turned to my mother, who looked away and quickly exited the ladies' room. My friend and I did not say a word. We left the ladies' room, and she went to the main sanctuary and I went back to the Bride's Room.

The ceremony was about to begin. My parents and I walked into a silenced sanctuary, and all eyes were on us. I kept my head down and felt so alone as we sat in our seats. On a warm, sunny day, the crowd looked smaller than had been present at Jane's funeral magnified by the size of the large sanctuary.

My parents had asked the rabbi to give the eulogy. I do not recall him speaking with us beforehand the way most rabbis would. His abominable eulogy centered on Margie's illness, not on Margie the individual. The eulogy should have been a tribute to Margie's life, but the rabbi focused most of the discussion on the perils of anorexia. He did not talk about Margie's wonderful character or qualities. *What about Margie as a daughter, sister, aunt, or friend?* Nothing. I was crushed, hurt, and angry by the insensitivity of the eulogy and the dishonor to Margie, which only added to my distress of the horrific day.

No one said anything to the rabbi afterward. My parents and I rode alone in the large, black limousine from the temple to the cemetery in thundering silence. When we returned to my parents' home—the house of shiva—I went upstairs to Jane's yellow room with windows that faced the street. I lay down on the bed. I felt so numb. Someone brought a delicious chocolate chip coffee cake, and it was the only thing I ate for days.

Margie was thirty-five when she died. She had been suffering from an eating disorder since she was sixteen. Reflecting on my loss, I realized that even though Margie's life had been on the line so many times and the end was near, her death was still shockingly traumatic. I had been losing my sister, piece by piece, for so many years, but nothing could have ever prepared me for her loss.

I sat up and placed my feet on the floor, worried that when I stood up I would lose my balance. I took a few deep breaths, then walked over to the window. I was anxiously awaiting the arrival of my daughters, who were with a babysitter, counting the minutes until their presence would help relieve my distress. Downstairs, a gathering of mourners chattered and ate, but I had no desire to be with them. No one noticed my absence.

I felt alone. Margie had died alone.

I regretted not seeing Margie one last time. My parents said she looked beautiful and was finally at peace, her face calm. But no one had offered me the opportunity to see her for myself. I felt invisible. Margie was my sister, yet I did not seem to matter.

No one seemed to care about how much losing her meant to me.

The last time I saw Margie, I had visited her with my daughters outside at the State facility. As not to scare the girls, I brought some toys for them to play with. Janie was four and Amy was three, so they were oblivious to their surroundings and were just happy to see their auntie Margie. The pictures of this day reflect Margie's ashen-colored face, emaciated frame, and blankness in her eyes. Her once-long, beautiful, silky hair was but a few mere straw strands. Janie and Amy provided the distraction, not much other conversation needed for the short visit. How I wish I could have seen my sister at peace.

After Margie's death, I struggled to hold myself together. *I have to be strong*, I thought. *What choice do I have?* I could not break into a million pieces. I was the sole surviving daughter of my parents and had two young daughters of my own to take care of. *Is this my life?* my voice shrieked inside my head. *How did tragedy strike our family not once, but twice?*

When my sisters died, the concept of being the sole surviving sibling seemed so foreign. It confused me. Anytime the focus landed on me, or my children, it felt strange and terrible, and even unconscionable. I preferred my own thoughts to hover in the background and to not occupy center stage. I did not know how to anchor myself without Margie and Jane.

I do not recall the exact timing, but I was never asked if I wanted any of Margie's mementos or keepsakes from her room. My mother, too sad, disposed of most of Margie's belongings from her pink bedroom. I wanted to hold close some treasures of my Margie—her pink Lucy poster from *Charlie Brown*, her Etienne Aigner handbag, or her white go-go boots. Somehow, by the grace of God, I did end up with her jewelry box that had multicolored drawers with white flower knobs, her pink desk chair, and her precious cheerleader necklace.

At an early age, Margie showed a sense of creativity and a flair for the dramatic. She used to drape a very long scarf over her head and body and wear a long beaded necklace. She loved bedecking herself in lots of garb and lipstick. Later, Margie showed her dynamic sense of fashion with white go-go boots, numerous stylish hats, and her signature precise application of black eyeliner, which she pulled off flawlessly. In most of her school pictures, Margie's straight hair was held back with a white headband, the fashion of the early sixties. She curled her gorgeous long, silky hair with large rollers and sat under a dryer. The dryer consisted of a big square plastic cover and a hose connected to a large base. Margie used to sit under the dryer for hours either in the big chair in my parents' bedroom or on her bed in the yoga "child's pose" position. Perpetually the actress, she loved drama. Margie creatively used pastels to draw, and she made unique cards to give to family members on birthdays and holidays. Her signature design was marked by hearts and balloons. Margie's effervescence overshadowed my quietness.

Margie always sent me cards, little books, and notes. I still cherish the Hallmark book she sent to me my first year in New York City. This poem cements the hole that is carved into my heart after I lost my sisters.

Thinking of You, Sister . . . and the Memories, Joy, and Love We Share

You're my sister, and I love you.

Every time I think of you, I smile just remembering all the good times we've had.

Sometimes I feel as if you're another "me."

You understand me so well and blend so perfectly with my changing moods.

When I'm with you, I know I can be myself.

You probably never realized how proud I am to have you for a sister.

When I mention you to someone else, it always makes me feel good to put "my sister" in front of your name.

When we're together, we always find things to talk and laugh about.

It's difficult to ever really know anyone,

But I think we know each other as well as two people can.

But you never try to change me, make me over into someone else.

You know how to encourage me and how to criticize me without hurting my feelings.

I don't know how you always find the right things to say, but I'm glad you do.

That's why I feel so glad and so lucky that I have you for a sister.

For so long, I knew in my heart that Margie's death was imminent, but the finality and reality was devastating and tragic. She fought a courageous battle for most of her life. I had lost and mourned a part of her for years, but now she was truly gone.

CHAPTER 3

Three Sisters

MEMORY: THE DIRECTOR ANNOUNCED, "THE LIPSON SISTERS WILL NOW SING 'SIDE BY SIDE.'" WEARING MATCHING DENIM SUNDRESSES, WE MARCHED IN A LINE TO THE STAGE TO PERFORM AT DAY CAMP. MARGIE STOOD IN THE CENTER NEAREST TO THE MICROPHONE, FLANKED BY JANE AND ME.

Three sisters. A trio, a triangle, a tripod, and a trilogy. Our stories are not what we dreamed but the sum of us, our genealogy, the Lipson girls.

Life began at the Lipsons on November 8, 1954, at 5:54 a.m. Marjorie Ellen Lipson was 7.25 pounds and 19.5 inches long, daughter of Benjamin and Eleanor Lipson.

Margie, the oldest of the Lipson girls, was the first golden girl. Her first home was the second story of a two-family house in a western suburb of Boston. The quiet residential street abutted a playground. I was born two years later on October 13, 1956, and our family moved to a single-story home in a wonderful, tight-knit neighborhood where we would live for fourteen years.

Photos of Margie in the earliest years reflected her constant smile, a bubbly and precocious personality, her dark, straight hair styled into a pixie cut with bangs, and big, dark brown eyes. I don't recall the early years, but in every photo, Margie was hugging me tight, gazing adoringly at her younger sisters or holding us close, our arms intertwined. When Margie was three, she and I would spend time in the wading pool in our backyard where she liked feeding me my bottle. Her straight hair contrasted to my curly hair, her lean frame to my chubby one.

Jane Esther Lipson was born on November 6, 1959. She was six pounds, seven ounces. My parents said I was elated at the arrival of my baby sister. Jane looked like a tiny bundle of beautiful, pink softness. The true baby of the family, she was absolutely adorable. With gorgeous locks of golden-blonde hair and a dimple on her right cheek, she was the apple of everyone's eye. When I put the baby pictures of my sister Jane and my daughter Janie side by side, the resemblance is uncanny.

Jane played the role of the youngest sister to the hilt. Margie and I doted on her. Jane quickly realized how to get her way. Her cute smile melted the hearts of everyone. If a fight ensued, Jane's crying on cue commenced the moment our parents entered the room, landing Margie and me in trouble.

I was the middle child, my secure identity. I possessed the true characteristics of a middle child: empathetic, with low self-esteem, someone who did not make waves, who disliked conflict, and who was unendingly flexible. This was not an easy placement of three girls born within five years—Margie two years older, and Jane three years younger. But knowing I had my sisters on either side of me, despite our differences and challenges, secured my foundation.

My first home was on Indian Ridge Road in a quiet suburban neighborhood of Oak Hill Park. I lived there until I was fourteen, and I have wonderful memories in that house. My sisters and I played hopscotch on the sidewalk as huge willow branches hung over to shade us. There was a fire alarm on a pole at the edge of the street. Every Sunday, my maternal grandparents, paternal grandmother, and great-aunt would come over for lunch, and they always parked their cars alongside the curb near our game so we'd have to stop playing. Excited to see them, we would jump over the grassy patch to open their car doors. We had a screened-in porch, a narrow room painted white, with a white sofa with blue and green flowers that glided back and forth where we played many board games.

It was a typical colonial house: living room, dining room, and staircase at the front door, which led up to three bedrooms and one full bathroom. Jane and I shared a bedroom. White furniture trimmed with gold, very sixties. We each had our own dresser and desk, and a shared nightstand stood between our beds. As the older sister, I admit that I did sometimes torture Jane by forcing her to stay on her side of the bedroom, but only for about fifteen minutes at a time. These were the only times I was able to control Jane's antics. If Jane was prevented from leaving the room, she could not get her way by crying. Our playroom was in the basement, which had black-and-white-checkered linoleum flooring, a black-and-white TV, games, toys, and Barbie dolls. At the bottom of the stairs to the right was a small room for my father's office. The laundry room and cedar closet was located at the far end of the basement.

The brick steps leading to the front door were rarely used except as the backdrop to countless photos. The side door had a breezeway with a metal box where the milkman delivered glass bottles of milk twice a week. We always entered through the back door and into the kitchen where the hubbub of our family life transpired—talking, eating, hanging out, playing games, doing homework. We had assigned seats around the white Formica table. I sat between Jane and my father, Jane next to my mother, and Margie between our parents. That kitchen table followed us for generations, even to my own home where I raised my daughters for many meals, snapshots, and gatherings.

In the backyard was a swing set and slide where we spent hours playing. My father attempted to teach the three of us to play baseball in the backyard, which proved fruitless. We had one ball, one bat, and one glove. The swing set was first base, the trees second base, the bulkhead third base, and a chair stood at home plate. From the pitcher's mound, my dad would throw underhanded pitches as we each took turns swinging the bat and missing the ball.

We were a close-knit community. I have fond memories of growing up in a secure, tight neighborhood where everyone played together. Neighborhood children were always in and out of each other's homes. The large gang of kids of varying ages shared the mile walk to the elementary school. On Monday, Wednesday, and Friday we came home for lunch then returned to school for the afternoon, and on Tuesday and Thursday school let us out at noon. Hebrew school met three days a week.

In kindergarten, four other girls and I rotated houses each day of the week. We played in the morning, had lunch, and ventured off to school. Our kindergarten class was a half-day, and it switched midway through the school year from morning to the afternoon session. All but one mother worked at home.

One morning, the five of us arrived to find the school grounds empty. We had dawdled along, not understanding how late we were. Mrs. Hodge, our unyielding kindergarten teacher with gray hair in a bun and black sensible shoes, stormed out of the building with a scowling expression and hollered at us.

She disciplined us for being so late. I remember shaking in my shoes.

I used to love to walk to school with my friends and sisters, but it was not as enjoyable in the winter. During one walk home from school, when I was eight and Jane was five, we had gotten out of school early because of the snow. It was a nor'easter blizzard snowstorm!

Jane insisted she could not walk in the deep snow. "I'm tired," she whined. "Carry me!"

My friend and I made a seat with our arms for Jane to sit upon, and we dragged ourselves through the pelting snow for the entire mile. The snow was piling higher, up to our thighs, making the excursion more arduous. Jane cried as we carried her. My feet hurt and were numb. My face was burning from the cold. When we finally arrived home, we were all cold and wet, and everyone was in tears.

As the middle of three girls, I often struggled to find my place because I was shy and introverted. What really helped pull me from my shell was going away to summer camp. I loved camp. I always looked forward to going away every summer. My sisters did not feel the same, however. Neither of them liked summer camp, but for very different reasons.

When Margie was nine, she would wake up crying because she repeatedly wet her bed. My parents would quickly change the sheets and comfort her. But Margie was mortified to have sleepovers with friends. When the problem persisted and eventually got worse and more frequent, my parents took her to Massachusetts General Hospital where she was diagnosed with a bladder malfunction that required major bladder surgery. All I recall is Margie bundled up in a white robe being pushed out of the hospital in a wheelchair that looked like a sled on wheels.

Margie recovered well and the bed-wetting stopped. The following year, Margie and I, at ages ten and eight, ventured off to Camp Fire Girls for two weeks. I counted the days to our departure. We packed the usual camp items like towels, toiletries, clothing, pedal pushers, rubbers (to keep our shoes dry from the rain), a deck of cards, and the navy Camp Fire vest with the beads of many colors—red, green, yellow, blue, and more—sewn on, representing the projects we had completed.

This was Margie's first attempt at a sleepover away from home, and it was not her forte. She hated being away from home, not sleeping in her own bed, and she was extremely homesick.

One day on our way to lunch, Margie grabbed me and started crying. "I hate everything! The food, the girls, and the activities!" she said.

When Margie cried, I cried.

"That's enough." The camp counselor pulled me away from teary-eyed Margie.

The following year, at age nine, I begged my parents to go away to overnight camp for eight weeks on my own, and they agreed. As the middle of three girls, that first year alone away at camp set the stage for patterns followed in years ahead. My need to disengage from my family provided me the opportunity to flourish.

It was June of 1966, and the day was warm and sunny. The parking lot at the Beethoven School in Newton was swarmed with eighty young girls, ages eight to sixteen, and their parents. We were waiting to take the four-hour bus ride to Camp Rapputak in Fryeburg, Maine. All the girls were outfitted in the required uniforms: a cobalt-blue short-sleeved blouse and navy-blue shorts, and a cobalt-blue stripe running vertically down the leg to match the blouse. The uniforms were not cheap, so my parents purchased a large size so it could last a few seasons. I remember all the girls feeling a huge sense of pride wearing the Camp Rapputak uniform, and I was excited for the adventure.

When two buses pulled into the parking lot, butterflies danced in my stomach. The older girls screamed with excitement, but I clung to my parents and started to cry. I wanted to go, but I was both overwhelmed and mesmerized by all the commotion and noise.

"Judy, you will be fine. Take your carsick medicine. Sit next to Maura, and remember to write us," my mother said as I boarded the bus, my cheeks wet with tears.

I had to be brave. After all, I'd begged my parents to send me away to camp. The director had visited our home and showed us all the beautiful pictures. How exciting to be on my own, just me, not pushed aside in the middle of three sisters.

The buses pulled out of the parking lot, and my parents were waving frantically as the squealing girls headed toward our eight weeks of fun. Would I be different at the end of the summer? Maybe taller, tan, a bit more grown up, and have experiences that remain shared and sacred.

For the next six summers, ages nine to fourteen, I went away to camp for eight weeks. My first four years, I boarded a bus solo to Camp Rapputak. The last two summers, Jane joined me and we switched to Camp Mataponi in Naples, Maine. My parents would come up on Visiting Day midway through the summer. I was never homesick, although I did cry the first year when they left on Visiting Day.

While I was away, Margie, the diligent correspondent, kept me apprised of all the goings-on at home, with a few exceptions. She sent me Polaroid photos of herself with as many notes and information on the back as she could cram in, but she didn't divulge family outings or adventures, like when they went to a show or visited Cape Cod. I found out about those types of things when I got home. I guess Margie didn't want me to feel like I was missing out.

There was one photo of Margie and Jane sitting on the brick steps in front of our home wearing Bermuda shorts, T-shirts, and flip-flops. Margie's long, straight brown hair was in pigtails, and Jane's cute, blonde hair is in a pixie cut with bangs. Jane sits knock-kneed with her elbows out to the side between Margie's knees. The endearing message on the back in Margie's handwriting reads, "This is known as a human totem pole (ha-ha). Have fun. Love Margie and Jane." How bright my day became when I received one of those photos!

When the time came for Jane to accompany me to overnight camp, I was thrilled. Jane was ten, and I was a seasoned camper at age thirteen. At last, a chance to have a little sister at camp. Jane was happy about it, too, because having a big sister at camp was a big deal, and she felt very special and important. When a younger girl visited her big sister's bunk, all the older girls made a fuss over her.

Jane insisted we visit Paragon Park, an amusement park in Hull, Massachusetts, on the cusp of Nantasket Beach, before we departed for camp. She did not want to miss out on the annual Lipson family pilgrimage to Paragon. The roller coaster, a monumental structure of white circular waves so tall it reached the sky, could be seen for miles away. Jane screamed with delight. Jane loved all the crazy rides like the roller coaster and Twister. My courage could only withstand the Ferris wheel and teacups. But cotton candy—a must for all. After what seemed like forever, we ate a dinner of fried fish and French fries with ketchup and headed home, only to return again the following year.

At camp, Jane took horseback riding and hated it. She came to my bunk every day in tears. I remember being annoyed. I was so happy to have my sister there, but all she did was complain and cry. *Did I really want to see her so much, and crying to boot?* After two weeks, we figured out all we had to do was tell the counselor Jane didn't like horseback riding and the ordeal would be over. The crying and visits ceased. A part of me missed the visits, and I still loved being a big sister at camp.

Going away to camp was an experience that influenced my life. Long-time friendships formed, life lessons learned, and fantastic exposure to numerous athletic skills. Looking back, the times in my life where I felt the most peaceful and happy mirrored my camp experience. I could be free, authentic, no comparison or judgment. I could just be Judy.

All through school, I always felt like I didn't belong. I should have been secure and confident in Judy, embraced her, but I did not.

Middle school presented a challenge for me. The faithful friends who formed the nucleus of activity in elementary school dispersed into new social groups, creating a larger, less centralized environment that was difficult to navigate. Unable to secure my own comfort zone or niche, I melted away. I felt lost in Margie's shadow and the path she forged with her own friends. I was never able to establish my own place. Margie's grandness was magnified by my smallness. But I loved her all the same.

A bat mitzvah is a coming-of-age ceremony for girls ages

twelve to thirteen. The special occasion is held in the synagogue on a Friday night during a Shabbat service where the daughter is blessed by her parents and the rabbi. Special prayers were bestowed, signifying her commitment to Judaism. Following the service, there's a celebratory dessert buffet of cakes and pastries for families and friends. Most celebrations continue with a kid's party held in a hall with a DJ and music. I went to many bat and bar mitzvahs in the late sixties. Boys would be clustered on one side of the room, and girls would congregate on the other side, all gawking at each other. Seldom asked to dance, often standing alone, I felt like a wallflower.

In 1967, a professional photographer came to the house to capture the milestone of Margie's bat mitzvah. Jane and I wore matching pink velvet short-sleeve dresses accessorized with pink pocketbooks with gold chain straps the length of the dresses. Margie, the girl of the hour, donned a different dress of raspberry pink with a white Peter Pan collar. Her typically straight hair was curled in a flip. Our outfits were completed by white fishnet stockings. Not to feel left out because of all the attention on Margie, my parents gave Jane and me a locket with a pink rose and our names engraved on the back. Each girl was photographed sitting on the needlepoint piano bench, oldest to youngest—the trio of three girls.

As with all sibling relationships, there were times of hurt feelings. Margie chose to exclude me from her bat mitzvah party—the exciting one with a DJ and dancing. A boy cousin a year older was invited, further exacerbating my hurt. I was left behind and felt devastated.

That night, I went to a sleepover at my cousin Betsy's house. Jane and Betsy—who were eight—were elated to have a sleepover with me. I slept between the two girls. We made popcorn and watched *Doctor Doolittle*. It was a real treat for them to stay up so late. To this day, I never understood why Margie left me out.

Two years later, in preparation for my own bat mitzvah, my mother took me shopping for a dress at Jordan Marsh, a large department store chain headquartered in Boston. Because I was chubby, I couldn't fit into regular sizes and had to shop in the half-size department. In a torturous process, I tried on more than fifty dresses. We finally settled on a yellow dress with white polka dots and long, sheer yellow sleeves that coordinated with the yellow-and-green color theme of my bat mitzvah. I left depleted, discouraged, and sad about the entire ordeal. My mother's attempts to say the dress was pretty did not cut it. It was not a happy time. There are no photographs from my bat mitzvah. I thought I looked horrible. After the Friday night service at the temple, we had a reception, but I did not have a kids' party with a DJ and dancing because I did not have enough friends to invite. I was the only Lipson sister who did not have a bat mitzvah party.

The family dynamic is such an interesting thing. My sisters and I each had our own unique relationships with each other and as a trio. There were fights, laughs, and tears, and we supported each other in many ways. When I think back on my teen years, I think I was just trying to find my way. We all were. Margie was outgoing, Jane was the goofball, and I was just somewhere in the middle, always wanting to be included, accepted, and loved.

On the year that each Lipson girl turned thirteen, our parents gifted us a charm bracelet for our bats mitzvahs. We personalized the charm bracelets over the years: Margie's bracelet was full of hearts, mine an eclectic assortment, and

Jane's held various souvenirs from the places we'd traveled. We loved hearing the clang of the charms as we moved, and felt an underlying competition about who had the most charms. At the time of this writing, I removed all of my original charms and wear just one large charm my father gave my mother. One side says, "We love you," and the other is engraved, "Margie, Judy, and Jane."

CHAPTER 4

Ice-Skating

MEMORY: DRESSED UP IN OUR SKATING GEAR, MY SISTERS AND I PUT ON OUR NEW RIEDELL SKATES FOR GROUP LESSONS AT BELLE ISLE SKATING RINK, EACH OF US RUSHING TO BE THE FIRST ONE ON THE ICE.

I began ice-skating at age eight with my sisters in group lessons at a small indoor rink, Belle Isle. Little did I know that a skating rink would set the stage for a lifelong passion. Never a competitor, I skated recreationally throughout my life. Surrounded by cousins and close friends, we had tremendous fun skating together. Margie, the natural athlete, was placed in the advanced group, I was with the beginners, and Jane with the kids her age.

From ages nine to eleven, I delighted in the thrill of dressing up in the skating gear of flesh-colored tights, a skating skirt, trunks that looked like heavy underpants to cover my tights, a wool sweater, and pretty gloves. After lacing up my skates, I'd step onto the cool, smooth ice. I stroked around to warm up, doing a crossover—crossing one foot over the other—around the corners of the large oval rink. The center was designated for ice-skaters practicing spins or jumps and individuals taking private lessons. Often, music played and we skated to its beat.

Margie and I took private lessons at the McHugh Forum rink at Boston College. Week after week, we proudly carried our Riedell skates in plaid skating bags. There was a pocket on each side of the bag designated for each skate, along with our skating guards and a rag to wipe off our wet blades. We sat on the green benches in the small waiting area that had a distinct odor from the college hockey players and laced up our skates. It was always a race and Margie usually won. Margie looked stunning in her dress barely covering her derrière, while my blue corduroy skirt was practically to my knees. Most skaters wore skirts or dresses at that time. My figure did not warrant a style like Margie's. Margie was the beautiful, graceful skater, while Jane and I chugged along. She did her jumps and spins without any effort. At times, I was jealous of Margie's ability and grace. Her coach wanted her to pursue the sport at the competitor level. Our parents decided against it because of the time and financial demands.

My timidity as a young girl transferred to ice-skating. I was never a powerhouse or a fast skater. One of the simplest, most basic jumps is a waltz jump consisting of a half rotation. To do a waltz jump, the skater takes off on the forward outside edge of the blade of one foot and lands backward on the outside edge of the blade of the other foot. Your leg is used as momentum— you kick it from front to back as you turn. When I was unable to complete this jump on my own, my extremely patient coach took my tentative hand and guided me through it. Petrified, I barely left the ice, but I remained grateful. Forty years later, I taught Learn to Skate lessons at the skating school founded by the coach who'd held my hand all those times.

As a family, we skated at the beautiful Larz Anderson Skating Rink (now the Jack Kirrane Skating Rink) in Brookline, overlooking Boston. My mother ice-skated with us for years.

She had a pair of Riedell skates. In her corduroy slacks, puffy jacket, and gloves, my mother, quite adept at ice-skating, stroked around the rink as my sisters and I took turns holding her hand, enjoying the lovely music heard throughout the rink. Even my father sported a pair of skates. That rink served the best hot chocolate to warm us after the brisk New England chill of ice-skating.

Breaking in new skates took weeks due to the stiff leather construction. We kept our old skates, as we were only able to skate in our new skates for a very short time, sometimes fifteen minutes to start. In our Lanz nightgowns, a hot hairdryer blew air to soften the leather, our skates laced, guards on, we watched television to expedite the process. We couldn't move around because the guards would ruin the carpet in the house. Needless to say, we held on to skates for as long as possible, not wanting to break the new ones in. Among the Lipson girls and friends, we had a hand-me-down circle for used skates.

Margie was a naturally gifted athlete. She attended a week-long tennis camp for two summers. As the smallest person on the cheerleading squad in middle school, Margie constantly practiced cartwheels and splits on the front lawn. Margie's skating career ended at age fourteen due to a heel injury. I don't think Jane was a huge fan of ice-skating and discontinued taking lessons after a few years. Jane did join Margie and me for public skating. Ironically, I was the one to continue.

I do not recall skating throughout middle school and high school, but I'm certain it remained a staple in my life. Throughout college, I skated at the rink near Skidmore College. I spent my free time at a rink close to the campus. Ice-skating remained a cherished outlet. I relished the escape from socializing, clearly not my strong suit. On the beautiful, slick ice, I felt free. It was only natural to have my college yearbook photo taken at the rink gliding down the ice. My leg was extended, one arm overhead, the other outstretched to the side. That was my happy place.

At Colgate University, where I spent a semester during my tenure at Skidmore College, I performed at halftime during a hockey game, skating to Bette Midler's "Boogie Woogie Bugle Boy." At five in the morning, my fellow skating club members and I trudged down a huge hill to the rink, practiced, and then trekked back up again. Wearing plaid skirts, white shirts, and ties, we skated to a real crowd pleaser.

My skating continued when I moved to New York City, but only recreationally. I enjoyed skating outdoors in Central Park and Rockefeller Center. Then my skating took a hiatus in the early years of motherhood, but I was thrilled to resume when my daughters started to skate. I took adult group lessons, and like riding a bike, skating was natural to me. The four adults in my class performed in front of the children at the end of the season. We had matching sweatshirts made—turquoise with a photo of a pair of skates. This was 2001, and in 2010 I actively resumed skating again with gusto.

As an adult skater, I'm always wondering what others think of me, and whether I look horrible out there on the ice. Another piece of letting go is judgment, and when I skate, those feelings I had as an outcast child start to surface. Sometimes it's difficult to let go of the negative thoughts and belief systems of my past. The truth is, people always tell me that I'm a pleasure to watch on the ice, and I try hard to believe them.

Over the years, as I ignored my grief, one thing always brought me back to myself: ice-skating. It wasn't until later when I realized that I was skating for me, Margie, and Jane, and how skating is a crucial centrifugal force that ignites a fire within me. We all ice-skated together, as young girls ages ten, eight, and five. Ice-skating was the thread that connected me to my sisters, but it was hidden in my subconscious for many years. My sisters' absences are felt deep in my heart—the fractured losses and the impact that cracked my life and my identity—but somehow ice-skating has held the pieces of me and my sisters together.

CHAPTER 5

Margie's Illness

MEMORY: IN PREPARATION FOR THE MOVE TO OUR NEW HOME, MY MOTHER GATHERED ALL OF US AROUND THE KITCHEN TABLE. "WHAT COLORS DO YOU WANT FOR YOUR NEW ROOMS?" SHE ASKED. MARGIE JUMPED UP AND YELLED, "PINK!" JANE SAID, "YELLOW." NATURALLY LAST, I SAID, "BLUE."

In the summer of 1970, Margie went to Israel for six weeks. She was sixteen. That was her first real length of time away from home. She traveled with a group her age and met one young girl from New York, and the two became close friends. They lived on a kibbutz, spent a weekend or two with an Israeli family, planted trees, and experienced the culture.

Upon Margie's return from the Israel trip, I knew something was amiss. When I came home from camp, Margie picked me up from the bus. In the car, so close, I was startled when I saw that her whole frame was smaller. We were both ecstatic to see each other after an absence of eight weeks, but Margie's bright sparkle had diminished.

"So, Lipson, how are you?" Margie said, almost in a forced manner. She'd nicknamed me "Lipson."

There was a different energy, I observed. A different Margie, though parts of her were still present. She had changed both physically and emotionally. She was thinner, and the sparkle and twinkle was absent from her eyes. She was fidgety and tapped her leg.

Was being away from home too much to handle? Did something happen in Israel that we did not know about? I remember thinking. Behind that smile, something was not right. Margie's challenging illness—anorexia and bulimia—all started after she returned from Israel.

That summer, our family moved from our childhood house into a larger home. Margie and I would be in closer proximity to our middle and high schools, but Jane was forced to switch schools in the sixth grade. Before we left for the summer, we each selected a color for our new rooms: Margie chose pink, I chose blue, and Jane chose yellow. All rooms were adorned with shag rugs, bedspreads, afghans made by Gram, and wallpaper covering ceilings and doors—all in coordinating colors.

After fourteen years, it felt strange to come home to new surroundings and not be in a room with Jane. Sharing a room with Jane for eleven years allowed us both a physical and emotional closeness. We used to sit next to each other at the dinner table, and we would walk to elementary school together every day. I missed being in the same room, choosing to talk or not talk, and just being together. It feels secure and comforting when your sister is right there with you. I missed the silly fights we'd have over who was going to turn out the light, and bumping into each other when we were getting something out of the closet. With separate rooms, that all changed. A distance formed.

In our old home, all of the rooms were next to each other. Our close bedrooms and one bathroom had given us an emotional closeness. There was no place to hide. In the new, larger house, there were more closed doors resulting in separation and fracture, especially for Margie. The new home had a long hall upstairs with Margie's room all the way down on the far end. My new room was a bit secluded, accessed by a tiny hallway. Furnished with a small television, my books, and the tools for needlepoint (a hobby I'd taught myself), my room was a place where I often retreated to find peace and turn off the noise of the household.

After the move, we went our separate ways. There was a distance between sisters. When Margie took off with her friends, I watched over Jane, but she no longer liked it anymore. Jane was older, asserting her independence, adjusting to her new school as a sixth-grader, trying to make friends, and engaging in typical pre-teen behavior.

Jane's friends took on a higher importance in her life than family. It took some time, but Jane eventually ensconced herself within the protection of many friends. This large group of friends provided her with an escape, a comfort, a diversion from facing challenging issues and decisions in her life. For Jane, surrounding herself with numerous friends secured a measure of happiness.

That year, Jane wrote an essay for her English class about moving to a new school at age eleven and navigating a new group of cliques. She was clearly upset about the move, sad about leaving her old friends, and nervous about making new friends. Jane always presented herself as confident, and she typically made friends wherever she went. I found it so superficial that it was heartbreaking to read. She stated only facts about her sisters, my and Margie's birthdates and school histories. But nothing with emotion or showing any endearing connection to us.

Looking back, I recognize that it must have been so hard on Jane to leave her friends and move to a new school. This was especially the case for Jane because she had some learning challenges. She needed to spend additional time studying to grasp the basic mechanics of most lessons. She lacked the discipline and drive. I suspect there might have been some learning disabilities not addressed in that era. Clearly, the move and Margie's illness impacted the entire family.

I was fourteen and in the ninth grade when Margie got sick. Some days, my parents would be off with Margie at either a doctor's appointment or visiting her in the hospital. I would walk directly home from school and dutifully do my homework. Jane arrived home around the same time. I would give Jane a snack and make sure she did her homework. We sat together at the round Formica kitchen table. By the time our parents walked in, I'd have dinner on the table.

Jane and I never talked about Margie or her anorexia and bulimia. We could have consoled and helped each other, but our family's constant code of silence and secrets prevented us from being open. We never knew how the other felt—if we were scared, angry, sad, or confused about the complexity of Margie's illness. Instead, we ventured to separate corners of our lives and rooms and never revealed our thoughts. Jane confided in her friends for diversion and comfort, constantly surrounded, and never wanting to be alone.

Doors closed. Relationships shifted.

I had few friends and was often alone. I didn't realize until I was older that I am a true introvert. Growing up, I was ostracized for not being social and outgoing in a family where that mattered. I did not fit the mold. I kept close to home and did not maintain a lively social life. In contrast, my mother and two sisters were outgoing, gregarious, and had socially assured personalities. Having a slew of friends was deemed important. At the appropriate age, securing a boyfriend was high in the ranks too. My mother never understood my incongruence to her, Margie, and Jane. What defined her did not define me.

We installed a second telephone line because the number of phone calls coming in from Margie's friends conflicted with my mother's social calls and my father's business calls. It was a big deal for Margie to get a telephone in her room, and eventually Jane got one too. It was not necessary for me, as I did not receive many calls. Margie would close her door and gab away for hours on her pink telephone, as did Jane years later.

To me, Margie was the "it" girl. She was popular, a cheerleader, never lacking for boyfriends, and before her illness, always had a cute figure. These were attributes I aspired to have, deemed important, and desperately wanted. Margie possessed the extrovert qualities opposite to my introvert qualities. She was a force to be reckoned with.

But everything changed in 1970 because my sister was struggling with a mental illness. For me, the situation was made worse by walking on eggshells and going out of the way to not talk about what was happening with my sister's eating disorder. Mental illness was a taboo topic in the seventies. The precarious nature of Margie's illness factored in as well. My parents did everything in their power known at the time for her treatment.

If I had a friend over, we'd sit in my room on the twin bed facing each other and talk about the frustrations of high school and the mean girls. Margie would come upstairs and awkwardly stand in the doorway, interrupting our conversation. Her thin legs constantly rocked back and forth. I felt so embarrassed and hurt at the sight of what my Margie had deteriorated into—and my dear friend would just chat away and try to engage Margie as best she could.

Jane and I could not tell anyone. We were kids. None of us had the capacity to cope with mental illness, especially at a time when it was such a socially prohibited topic. It was a subject nobody talked about. Jane and I didn't even talk to each other about it, nor did we feel we could. All those years Margie suffered, we were like robots going through the motions of our lives. Jane and I never even knew much about Margie's illness. Some days our lives were quite normal while other days were a tsunami of chaos. The "routine" of our lives was constantly disrupted despite our best efforts to soldier on.

I spent the summer of 1971 at a prep school in Western Massachusetts. The gorgeous school looked like something out of a movie with its beautiful brick buildings and lush grounds. The program included courses on literature and the history of jazz. I slept in a neat attic dorm room with a slanted ceiling. My roommate hailed from another town in Massachusetts. I relished being away from my family, away from the drama, and being able to be myself without having to divulge or explain my family history.

At some point, I received a letter from home that set me off. It probably was about Margie being in the hospital again. Over the past year, Margie had been in and out of the hospital for her eating disorder, and she had taken off a lot of time from school. When I received that letter, I retreated into silence, shut down, and stopped talking to others. This became my pattern. I was unable to understand or talk about Margie's illness and equally unable to communicate my thoughts or feelings.

The precariousness of Margie's illness, the unknowns of her

treatments, forced us all into a life of uncertainty. When would there be a crisis? What would the next call bring? How long would the hospital stay be? When Margie was doing okay and was on level ground, we wondered when the shoe would drop. It was always just a matter of time.

We tried a few fatal attempts at family therapy in the early stages of Margie's illness. The sessions were daunting. I remember that first therapy session. There were five chairs arranged in a circle—one for each family member, excluding Margie, and a chair for the therapist. I spent the hour looking down at the floor. Jane fidgeted in her chair. The social worker's efforts to facilitate our family's discussion were fruitless.

"How do you feel?" the social worker had asked. I had no clue. *Feelings* was a foreign word to Jane and me, and we glared at the social worker with pouty faces refusing—or unable—to answer. Immense silence permeated the cold room.

The social worker tried again. "What do you feel about your parents?"

No response.

"Girls, speak up," said my parents.

Still no response. For the rest of the abbreviated session, my parents and the social worker exchanged a few words, but Jane and I remained mute.

I think we were forced to attend one more session, clearly not a productive exercise. We scurried out as quickly as possible when the hour was complete. Family therapy was another secret I could not share with anyone. Jane and I never discussed the therapy.

After that, Jane and I shut down. Neither knew what the other felt about Margie or our parents. Jane was still adjusting to a new school and neighborhood. I was busy with school and taking care of everyone, making dinners, and washing laundry.

This was the beginning of a time of my life when I was just go-go-go. There was no time for thinking, just running and running through my life.

Margie was in and out of school. Her appearance had drastically changed. My parents had bags under their eyes and often appeared tense. Vicious rumors spread, including that Margie did drugs. "Where is she?" people asked. "What is wrong with the parents?"

One day during my sophomore year, I was standing at my locker putting my books away when a group of girls passed by. Out of the corner of my eye, I could see fingers pointing at me.

"She's the one," said a girl smacking on chewing gum. "It's her sister—remember that cute cheerleader? She's sick."

"She's in the nut house," chirped the one with the bopping ponytail.

"Probably drugs," the third girl said.

My face turned red; my body froze. It took all my self-control not to cry. The words hurt me to the core. When the bell rang, I closed my locker. Shoulders slumped, head down, I slid into my assigned homeroom seat. I went about my day barely able to focus. I said nothing. And I never told a soul.

Most of the time I kept my head down as I walked the halls amid stares, glares, and blatant gossip. My history teacher, who had given Margie an A two years earlier, gave me a better grade than I deserved. Though I suppose she was trying to show empathy and compassion, it bothered me that she changed my B average to an A minus.

That year, Margie and I spoke as often as her hospitalizations and my school schedule would allow. She was a diligent correspondent, sending notes, cards, and little books. She wanted to be apprised of my life and how I was doing, and we talked about our parents. Being together remained as natural as it could be. I wanted, hoped, and longed for her to get well. Yet, there seemed to be one disappointment after another. Conversations in person were awkward at best.

"Hey, Lipson, how's school?" Margie would ask. "What are Mom and Dad saying about me?"

"School's okay. I hate biology, I love my English class, Miss Malone is great," I'd answer. "Mom and Dad don't say much about you."

"I can't wait to get out of here." To that I did not respond.

Phone conversations were easier. When I visited my sister in the hospital, my nerves escalated. As a teenager, I visited Margie in a psychiatric hospital, not knowing the details of her illness. Although I have a terrible sense of direction, I somehow instilled in my brain the driving directions from our house to McLean Hospital in Belmont, Massachusetts. I can still see the Route 16 sign in my mind.

I often felt overwhelmed by the idea that my sister Margie was in a psychiatric hospital. At times, Margie's behavior grew disruptive, erratic, or edgy. When I visited her, I did not know, from one hour to the next, what I was going to get. I brought her reading material: *Seventeen* and *Life*, the *Boston Globe* and the *Boston Herald*. Margie was a voracious reader. I also brought pads of paper and pastels for her to create cards.

The burden of not telling anyone about Margie was exhausting and caused me to revert further into my shell. As a bashful child, making conversation and opening up had been a constant struggle. Protecting our family's secrets magnified the struggle. My communication skills often faltered because I was always horrified that I might reveal or say something forbidden.

My mother played mahjong with a group of women every week. The daughter of one of the women was my age. One day, the girl saw me walking to school and tried to befriend me. I did not let her in. With so many family secrets, I put her off and kept to myself. It was the only way I knew how to be.

When I turned sixteen, I had few close friends and no desire for a party. To mark the milestone, my mother prepared a special dinner and bought a cake from a local bakery. Jane, my parents, and I sat down to dinner in the dining room, which our family reserved for holidays and special occasions. The table was set with the good china, tablecloth, and candles.

After dinner, before the cake with candles came out, and before they could sing "Happy Birthday," the telephone rang. My father dashed to answer it—a crisis about Margie. Jane and I, as always, were in the dark. My parents left us at the table. *Happy sweet sixteen, Judy.*

Thirty years later, I found out that Jane's bat mitzvah in 1972 had to be postponed from November to March because Margie was in the hospital. I have no recollection of it. The family photographs reflect a mood of doom and gloom. Not one family member looked happy or was smiling. Jane and I had never talked about it. I think it was a memory I blocked out.

Our hearts broke when Margie was unable to participate in her high school graduation. She was so disappointed. All of her friends were making preparations and going to the prom, but Margie did not have the physical or emotional capacity to attend. Despite her numerous absences from school in her junior and senior years, Margie did manage to graduate. But receiving her diploma in the mail was no match for being present at her graduation. Margie attended Simmons College in Boston for a few months for her freshman year, but was unable to continue.

When the time came for me to apply to colleges, my decision, without a doubt, was to study out of state. My parents were preoccupied with Margie's illness, and they could not focus on helping me find a college to fit my needs as a shy, introverted girl. My parents skimmed through the process based on one meeting I had with a guidance counselor.

My first visit to Connecticut College sealed my vision that it was the ideal college campus. It was like a scene out of a movie—in my mind, the one and only place to be. I was crushed when I was rejected both in early- and regular-decision cycles. I ended up at Skidmore College in Saratoga Springs, New York.

In the meantime, Jane had been experiencing her own academic struggles. She had trouble spelling and writing sentences. She forgot to study. As early as 1968, there had been requests for my parents to reinforce learning and to practice math and reading with Jane. Her middle school teachers all commented that Jane lacked discipline, socialized too much, was unprepared for class, and was unwilling to seek extra help when advised to do so.

My parents sent Jane to a private school for her freshman and sophomore years of high school, hoping it would help with her schoolwork, and also set her on the right track and off her wild streak. The school was not the right fit, and Jane returned to public school for her junior and senior years. Looking back, I don't think any school would have done the trick. Jane needed someone to talk to, to guide and support her. But the distraction of Margie's illness prevented any focus on Jane.

There was a point in 1975 when Margie was "functioning" for a time and we vacationed in California. That was our last trip together as a family. Some of my fondest memories with Margie and Jane were during that trip. We visited Los Angeles, drove up the coast to San Francisco, went to Disneyland, saw Judy Collins in concert, met Alan Hale Jr. who played the Skipper on *Gilligan's Island*, and had many fights, but even more laughs.

Margie and I snuck Jane, underage at sixteen, into a comedy club. The crowded third-rate establishment had tables and chairs packed close together with barely enough room to walk in between, and an elevated stage lit in contrast to the darkened audience. I'm not sure why we arrived late, but that was all comedian Eddie Murphy needed to make us a part of his act.

The jokes about us began. *Do we continue to our seats or stand and take the wrath of Eddie Murphy?* Mortified, we slumped in our seats. The darkened room prevented others from seeing our bright red cheeks. Once we got over the humiliation, the Lipson sisters giggled. What a great story to tell!

That vacation was a great distraction, but once we returned to the East Coast, things fell right back into place and reality set in. Another year passed. While Jane struggled in high school, I was away at college and came home for the summer. The summer of 1976, Margie was functioning for a time—living in her own apartment in Brookline. With great entrepreneurial spirit, she secured a cart at Faneuil Hall and sold antique fashion magazine covers. The business was more of a hobby to keep her busy.

That year, Margie and I attended the Boston Pops Bicentennial Fourth of July Concert on the historic Boston Esplanade. After the concert, we took in the sensational fireworks display and could not stop people watching.

"Lipson, check out that patriotic outfit—they went all out!" said Margie.

"Can you imagine wearing that?" I could not stop laughing.

"Why not? You would look great."

"Margie, stop, I'm going to wet my pants. And I'm not going into those porta potties!"

I felt unbounded excitement at being together, not yet

knowing that the next month Margie would have a medical emergency, and the following month another hospital visit.

I was grateful to be away during my college years from 1974 to 1978. I majored in business with a concentration in marketing and accounting, hoping for a career in banking. In addition to my Skidmore classes, I worked all four years, mostly in the admissions office providing tours to potential students. I made few friends but went with the flow, continually still worried about Margie's ups and downs and hospitalizations, and Jane's tense relationship with my parents because of her "wild side."

Every week, I took the bus from Saratoga Springs to Albany and then rode another bus to New York City for job interviews. As backup, I interviewed for retail positions. One interview stood out.

Macy's Department Stores called me in for an entire day of interviews. For part of the day, eight interviewees sat in a room and were given an employee personnel folder. Seated behind us were four Macy's executives. The task for the group of eight was to decide which of the employees was to be promoted. One person in the group took charge; others spoke up. I sat silent. That was the scariest form of an interview. I did not get the job. I received no offers from the banks. But still, I was lucky.

Bloomingdale's hired me.

CHAPTER 6

New York City Girl

MEMORY: "GIRLS, COME INTO THE DEN!" MY MOTHER CALLED, PLACING THE 33 SOUNDTRACK OF *THE SOUND OF MUSIC* ON THE RECORD PLAYER. MARGIE, JANE, AND I SANG ALONG AS MARY MARTIN CROONED "DO-RE-MI" AND "EDELWEISS" SO WE COULD LEARN ALL THE LYRICS BEFORE WE WOULD SEE THE SHOW.

I moved to New York City in August of 1978. My father sent me off with parting advice. "Judy," he said, "there will be days when you love it, days when you hate it, but you must roll with the punches." These words solidified in my brain, and I have referred to them over and over in my life.

In my final summer before embarking on my real-life career, I worked at a day camp for six weeks and prepared for the big move to New York City. I was hoping to spend time with my sisters before I left, not knowing what my new life would bring.

My nerves and anticipation heightened as I planned my big move to New York City. I was twenty-one, and there was a new independent streak in me. I had never before done anything like this. Margie and Jane were floundering in their lives, and I was about to embark on an exciting chapter in mine.

My sisters and I planned a twenty-fifth anniversary party for our parents two days before my departure. Margie, the boss, insisted on refreshments upstairs and a dance party in the basement. She loved to dance. All of my belongings were packed in the basement, and we could not have a dance party unless I moved my stuff to the storage room, which had water damage. I went ballistic, but the oldest sister always got her way. In the end, I caved. The party was a smashing success. We all wore pink carnations in our hair and smiles from ear to ear. It was one of the last times we were all together—and one of the happiest.

Years later, I found a poem I had written for my parents' anniversary. I had been spot-on in defining each Lipson girl.

Margie is the oldest of your three charming girls,
    and with her disco dancing she swings and twirls.
She is the salesgirl of the crew
    whose humor and charm are held through and through.
Off on her own to open a new business cart,
    how about an original antique print to start?
Her calls are enjoyed all the day,
    dialing Daddy in her own way.

Judy is the middle one,
    like her mother, organized in getting things done.
The two look the most alike,
    and both do needlepoint with all their might.
Judy goes on her new venture in life,
    hoping to give Bloomingdale's a new spice.
Being in the middle is not always an easy space,
    but in Judy's life, both sisters hold a very special place.

Jane is the youngest of the crew
    whose voice is heard through and through.

She talks on the phone all day
 to keeps tabs on everyone in her own way.
At Fessenden, Jane holds a special place,
 keeping all the campers in their happy face.
Another Lipson disco queen,
 how about a new dance to screen?

Before I left for New York, Jane surprised me. Most conversations I had with Jane were mainly superficial. But that time her eyes filled up with tears and she hugged me. "Judy, I am proud of you." She handed me a card. "I love you."

In the card, Jane wrote a note at the bottom in her own words: "Our relationship is very important to me. At times I don't seem to show it. I am happy that we can accept each other for who we are. I love you dearly, and whenever you need me, just call. I am always here. Best of luck."

"Back at you, my sister," I said. I cried and we hugged again.

Living in New York City at twenty-one was undoubtedly the happiest time of my life (with the exception of giving birth to my children). I was young, naïve, anxious to start my retail career, and ready to take the world by storm. I lived in a two-bedroom apartment with three other girls, all Skidmore graduates. Two were nurses on opposite schedules from mine, and the other was an art student at Pratt. I drew the last straw so my room was a piece of the living room sectioned off. I worked grueling hours on a meager salary, yet loved being on my own away from family. No one knew my history.

Bloomingdale's—one of the most famous department stores, with its fast-paced hustle and bustle—was my place of employment. I could hardly believe it. I'd leave at night only to find the store reconfigured the next day with a revived, new, vivacious look. Trying to navigate the ins and outs of the operations, personalities, and politics of a large organization was very different from living in my college cocoon. I made new friends who were starting careers, all of us with our eyes wide open, aware of our naïveté.

One of the highlights of living in New York City was skating on the ice rink at Rockefeller Center, which was always so beautifully decorated for the holidays. Walking down to the rink, I took in the white angels and elegant Christmas tree with countless sparkling lights. In my first winter in New York City, I realized that skating on an outdoor rink, especially this one, was exquisitely freeing. Tourists crowded in, dying to experience ice-skating firsthand at the famous Rockefeller Center. The energy was vibrant, and the skating, people, and holiday cheer felt enchanting.

After that first grueling 1978 Christmas season in retail, Jane and I planned a trip to Aruba in March 1979. The vacation is a blur now, but the pictures show us tanned with glowing smiles. The trip was right up Jane's alley—there were no pressures, and she was away from the restrictions of curfews of living under our parents' roof. The drinking age was eighteen in Aruba, so Jane lived it up. Looking back, I am eternally grateful for that precious time together two years before she died.

Although I was physically separated from my parents in college and New York City, there was always this feeling of a double existence when it came to family—a feeling of push and pull, the life that I wanted versus the reality of my life. I had a certain life before my sisters' deaths and a different life after. And in between there was a life after Jane died while Margie was still alive but sick. *Who was I and what was my role?* No answers ever lasted long in those years. Everything felt confusing.

In my dreams, I always imagined arriving home and walking through the door to an immediate scuffle as my sisters and I argued over who would take the car for the afternoon. I pictured the three of us watching the black-and-white television in the basement, playing on the swings in the backyard, or wearing matching outfits on a trip to Florida. The scenes in my mind went on and on. But my dreams were squashed and reality hit.

Jane's death came as such a shock in 1981. I was thriving in New York, loving my life, my living situation, and my job. But it all came to a crashing halt.

I was twenty-five years old when Jane died—a precarious age at a time when my own personal growth was thrown into a volcanic wave of loss.

During that first hectic Christmas season at Bloomingdale's, I met my husband who worked in operations. Our lives crossed paths for four years, and we married in 1983. The marriage was short-lived. He had been kind to me after Jane died, but unfortunately, my decision to marry was made at a vulnerable time that was clouded by my inability to acknowledge, express, or channel my grief and emotions over losing my sister.

My parents had coerced me to see a therapist in New York City. She was a plump woman with gray hair knotted into a bun, which reminded me of my kindergarten teacher who I'd considered mean and horrible. Her gray skirt was oddly hiked up beneath her bra, and the ensemble was topped off with a white blouse.

The therapist's apartment resembled that of an absent-minded professor with piles of books and papers scattered everywhere. I do not know what I said to this woman or what we talked about, but every time I said a word, she would scribble it on a legal pad with a yellow pencil, never once maintaining eye contact. I imagine I cried. How could I not? The therapist was clueless to validate or understand the impact of my loss. I went for a handful of sessions. She provided neither comfort, nor guidance, to a shattered girl in desperate need of someone to hold her hand. I quit the unproductive process fairly quickly.

In the early years, Jane and I were inseparable. This was evident in our childhood photographs—Jane and I, always side by side. My Jane, with her blonde bob and darling face. Jane looked up to me and depended on me, and I cherished having a little sister. We bickered like all siblings do, but we mostly got along. I have fond memories of our yearly vacations at the Summer's End resort in Maine. Me and Jane, in our camp uniforms, and sitting in the backyard. Clearly happy to be with one another as evidenced by our smiles.

One vacation in Maine, Jane and I wore matching bathing suits with white hooded cover-ups. We looked like identical twins holding paper plates with barbeque and corn on the cob next to a picnic table with a red-and-white tablecloth. Another snapshot showed us a few years later at the same resort standing on a dock near the lake. My arm was draped over Jane's shoulder, and her arm was secured around my waist. We stood on chubby legs, knees knocked together. All those years ago, I never realized how much Jane and I resembled each other, nor how close we were in childhood.

My heart longed for my sisters. I wanted Jane alive, wanted Margie well—and later, I wanted Jane *and* Margie alive. After Jane died, I stayed with my parents for the week. The phone would ring constantly and my parents would become irreparably distracted. Or they would leave home for an interminable amount of time. It was a difficult time for many reasons, and Margie had been committed to yet another psychiatric hospital.

Here we go again, I thought. I'd lost track of how many times she'd been hospitalized, how many times we'd felt the same deep anguish. A few weeks after Jane's death, I visited Margie, despairing that the state facility was not as nice as the private ones, but after so many years, options were running out. I held back tears as we sat outside on two metal chairs. Margie was painfully thin, fidgety, and edgy. Her eyes were deep and sunken.

The visit was terrible and I kept it short. Anger, frustration, and sadness wore on both of us after over a decade of trying to cope. "I'm doing better," Margie said. "Tell Mommy and Daddy to get me out of here." For the first time she did not ask, "Lipson, what's new?" The loss of our sisterly "code" was devastating. I left distraught. For months afterwards, I did not see and barely talked to Margie. I could not handle the ups and downs, the ins and outs, the loss of my older sister.

My mother often reminded me that she had cried every day for two years after Jane died. I don't think she forgave me for returning to New York City shortly after Jane's death. But what was I supposed to do? Move back home with my parents? These types of questions weighed on me over the years, but I don't regret going back to New York. I couldn't give up my new apartment and new job promotion. I was twenty-five years old, had just lost one sister, and my other sister was fighting for her life.

From 1978 to 1985, I lived in New York with a brief hiatus to Washington, DC, from 1980 to 1981 for a promotion from Bloomingdale's. I look fondly back at my years in New York. The Bloomingdale's Executive Training Program afforded me numerous opportunities and allowed growth professionally and personally. The work was grueling but exciting and fun. The shy, young twenty-one-year-old became more confident over the years, her eyes opened to a whole new world. New York is a city that never sleeps. It was a perfect escape from the reality I did not want to face.

CHAPTER 7

Generations

MEMORY: WHEN OUR FATHER ARRIVED HOME AFTER A LONG DAY, WE WERE EXCITED TO TELL HIM THAT OUR MOTHER BAKED HIM A CAKE. "WHAT KIND?" HE ASKED. MY SISTERS AND I CHIMED IN, "DUNCAN HINES!"

In 1985, the birth of my first child in New York was a blessing for the entire family. If the baby was a girl, I wanted to name her after Jane. Thankfully, my parents were on board. The way I carried made me certain I was having a boy. I never told a soul how much I wanted a girl because, above all else, I wanted a healthy baby. Surprise, surprise! Jane Esther, whom we call Janie, arrived on her exact due date. My mother knitted Janie a hat and matching sweater she wore home from the hospital. For me, my daughter's inheritance of Jane's name ensured that my sister was always with us and would always live on. Eighteen months later, we happily welcomed our younger daughter, Amy.

After Margie died in 1990, I got sucked back into the family fold. When Janie turned six months old, I moved back to Boston because I felt that my parents needed her in their lives. After being away for almost a decade, I now felt an obligation to fill in the two vacant spaces left by my sisters. As a result, day by day, my own identity started to be chipped away.

The impact of my sisters' deaths affected both generations. My mother's dreams of having a large family were shattered, and she tried to recreate her family through my daughters and me. But what we all needed was to rediscover our own identities. Who were we without Margie and Jane? What paths would we forge now? We needed to move forward, not try to make up for our losses.

For my parents, the pain was too intense so we rarely broached the subject of my sisters. Taking the lead from them, I never mentioned Margie or Jane. My parents were extremely helpful to me as a single, working mother with two children. I worked part-time and received my master's degree in library science. I ran a small corporate library for seven years in close proximity to home. But some days I felt an obligation to always involve my parents when I just wanted to be home alone with my two daughters.

My life was hectic at that time raising two daughters on my own, working, and chauffeuring my daughters to after-school activities. Our house resembled a sorority with lots of laughter. I had to be very organized—backpacks loaded the prior night and lunches made, all lined up for the ready so we could sit down in the morning to a calm breakfast before the day began. No telephone calls received during dinner where we sat down as a family recapping our days. Music was a staple in our home with numerous dance parties in the living room. Our house was filled with people, entertaining for Shabbat dinner, holidays, birthday parties, and barbeques.

Our Shabbat dinners with my parents and daughters were reminiscent of my childhood. On Friday nights, we often had Shabbat dinner at our grandmother's home, and my sisters and I would play in the living room before dinner. Grandmother

Ethel, whom we called "Gram," prepared the traditional meal with chicken soup, chicken, kugel, and her delicious goodies for dessert. Grapes were always a staple at dessert time. One Friday night, the grapes were absent.

"Why?" Jane asked my grandmother.

"The grapes were too expensive this week," Gram answered. My grandmother, forever the saver, would travel to three supermarkets to save five cents on cottage cheese. The following week, the grapes appeared on the table.

Jane piped up. "Grandma, I see the cheap grapes!"

When we were younger, our parents liked to travel once a year for a weekly getaway, and Gram would stay with us. We girls were always on our best behavior—barely any fights. I'm sure it was not easy taking care of the three of us, but we loved it and I'm sure Gram did too. It's crazy to think about, but we managed the entire time without a car.

On Saturday mornings, we would all snuggle together in the king bed in our parents' room and watch cartoons, then shuffle downstairs for a late breakfast. Gram was a fabulous cook and baker. She made the best strudel with her long, thin rolling pin; we ate golden raisins and helped her. Everything she made was delicious. She let us frost the chocolate cake and lick the spoons. Gram never measured anything. A juice glass served as a cup, a teacup served as a cookie cutter, a coffee spoon her teaspoon— she utilized whatever she could find in the kitchen.

Gram crocheted afghans for all of us in the colors of our bedrooms—pink for Margie, blue for me, and yellow for Jane. When I went off to college, she made a granny square afghan for the bed in my dorm room using the Red Heart yarn she bought at Woolworth's. Gram had us take turns holding our arms outstretched so she could roll her yarn. Her attempts at teaching us how to crochet proved fruitless, but it was always fun.

Another tradition was our Friday night surprise. Our father worked long hours in the insurance business, and we were always glad to see him. But Friday evenings were special. As our father pulled into the driveway, the three of us would dash out to greet him because he always had something special for us—usually candy, or for a special occasion, a doll. He continued the tradition with his grandchildren, stopping by on Friday mornings with challah and cupcakes for my delighted daughters.

My daughters are my world. Their relationship often reminds me of that bond I shared with my sisters. My daughters are kind, caring, and have a great sense of humor, just like me and my sisters. There was always a playful silliness with the Lipson sisters. I'll never forget the first time I babysat Jane. I was in sixth grade and Jane was in third. Jane had brought home a hamster from school for the weekend. We sat in our parents' room in the big, comfy chairs watching television.

I heard a chirp-chirp-chirp sound. I said to Jane, "Quiet, do you hear that?"

"No, I don't hear that," Jane said.

"Quiet, listen, how can you not hear that? What is that noise?"

"Oh yeah, maybe."

"Turn off the TV," I yelled at Jane, and she did as she was told. "Now can you hear it?"

"Yes," her voice quivered.

Scared out of my mind, I grabbed Jane's hand and we peeked into the hall and heard the chirping noise repeatedly. The two of us screamed and shut the door. Jane and I huddled together on the floor. Again, the chirp-chirp-chirp noise sounded. When we finally got our wits about us, we realized the noise was coming from the hamster downstairs. The two of us could not stop laughing.

Another funny memory I have is when Margie was ten and I was eight. We went snooping for Chanukah presents in the basement in my father's office. Typical of our relationship, Margie was the boss. When we opened the door to the basement, I wanted to chicken out.

"Margie, we can't do this. We're going to get into trouble."

Margie smirked. "Come on, Judy, no one will know. It will be our secret—promise you won't tell?"

"I promise," I said.

As we crept down the steep linoleum stairs to our father's study—Margie first, then me—we pinky swore never to tell. We stood in the front of the door for a moment, then Margie twisted the knob and pushed it open. Sure enough, the presents were stacked on the desk. We quickly rushed over and squealed with excitement over the large boxes and stifled our laughter so we wouldn't get caught.

Margie grabbed a medium-sized box and carefully started peeling the tape off the corner.

"Margie! What are you doing? They'll know we opened them," I gasped. I thought we were just on the hunt for the presents, not knowing that she had intentions to open them.

"Don't worry, you scaredy-cat," she giggled. Then she continued to peel the paper back.

"How are we going to rewrap them?"

"Look, the tape peeled right off," said Margie. "We'll put them back just as we found them."

My heart pounded as I watched her pull back the paper to reveal the name underneath. It was an Easy-Bake Oven. I was so excited, and together we peeled back the tape on all of the presents: Creepy Crawlers and button-making toys, which were the cat's meow.

For Chanukah, the presents were placed at our assigned seats at the dining room table. As we each opened one present, Margie and I acted surprised. "Wow, just what I wanted. Thank you so much!" We ran to give our parents a kiss. Our performances were worthy of an Oscar award. Margie eyed me with a twinkle in her big brown eyes. My non-poker face did not give us away. We held this secret between us until decades later when it was finally revealed to our parents.

I love those types of memories—so carefree and innocent. When I became a mother and watched my daughters grow up together, it reminded me so much of me and my sisters.

I had so wanted my daughters to ice-skate, just like the Lipson girls did so many years ago, but it didn't take right away. They wanted to rollerblade instead. One spring my daughters and I decided to try rollerblading. The girls were eleven and twelve. For some reason the scheduled lesson had a mix-up, so the instructor came to our home to provide the lesson. Geared up with helmets, kneepads, and elbow pads, off we went circling the neighborhood. Being a skater, I took to rollerblading fairly well and the girls did too. Not so easy to stop, we slid into the grass. The instructor wanted me to advance and attempt the hills on Beacon Hill. I passed. Our roller blades surfaced a few more times but mainly collected dust in the garage.

Life continued on, as it always does. The dust was settling a bit, and I'd gotten into a routine with my family. Then, in the fall of 1995, my daughter Amy, age ten, broke her knee and was in a cast from her ankle to the top of her thigh. Instead of our annual apple-picking outing, we strolled into Bloomingdale's where I ran into an old colleague. We hugged, laughed, and told my daughter of our times together during our twenties as department managers in the Bloomingdale's Virginia stores. The two of us had co-chaired an executive outing to a crab restaurant in Maryland. He proposed I come back to work at Bloomingdale's.

"How can I work retail?" I said. "I'm a single mother with two daughters in school."

"We will make it work."

I called my father, who always provided excellent advice. He listened carefully, as he always did. "Judy, in business I've learned two theories," he said. "Go with your gut and your instinct."

I took his words seriously and returned to Bloomingdale's. Whenever I feel confused about making a decision, I always think of my father's words: *Trust in yourself. Trust in your decisions.*

For the next ten years, I went back to my roots working full time at Bloomingdale's in Chestnut Hill. I was thirty-nine and working in Bloomingdale's full time. I was focused on raising Janie and Amy, and being there for my parents. In addition, I became involved with the temple. The girls kept me busy with their schedules, being the sole parent. I did not divulge my history of losing two sisters to new people I met. Hearing individuals speak about their siblings always felt like a knife in my heart, but I always smiled and listened. Memories of Margie and Jane in my subconscious yet remained at the foremost of my heart.

I started noticing that pieces of memories were coming alive. For years I had suppressed so much, but something was calling to the surface from my subconscious to my conscious mind. I would get snippets of memories seemingly for no reason.

One day, I was walking around the lake and passed a young couple that was decked out in Red Sox gear. I smiled and thought of my father. Our family loved the Boston Red Sox. Avid baseball fans, we held two season tickets for many years. I was elated when game seven of the 1967 World Series was set in October in Boston, and I was chosen over Margie and Jane to attend because it was my birth month. Seated on the first-base side, I watched Jim Lonborg pitch. Unfortunately, the Red Sox lost to the St. Louis Cardinals, 7–2, but even so, witnessing history at an October World Series game at Fenway Park—the ultimate Boston experience—was unforgettable. My father and I had the best time. Whenever these memories popped up, I always embraced them.

I made it my mission that my girls had good, happy, and healthy experiences and memories. I wanted them to be close, just like me and my sisters were. My Margie was always so encouraging, and I felt like she was always looking out for me, even when she really needed to look out for herself.

Over the years, I'd started several needlepoint businesses. Margie had brilliantly named the one I started in college "Julip," combining my first and last names. In 1987, a friend and I launched a new venture, a needlepoint business we called Needlepointers. Margie understood its importance to me, and I will never forget how supportive she was when she called me on opening day.

"Lipson, I want to wish you the best of luck," Margie said.

Stunned, my eyes filled with tears. *How did Margie remember the date?* I thought. The call only lasted a minute, as Margie was calling from the state hospital. Yet, her sisterly love was true to form, and not for the first time, I thought, *She is truly my champion.*

One of the biggest hurts is that my daughters don't know their aunts. They'd never met Jane, and they were very young when Margie was still alive. Margie loved being an aunt, and she established an immediate connection of warmth and love with my girls. She held them and hugged them. Her illness was a non-issue for the girls. Margie loved being present for her nieces. Her only wish was to babysit, but sadly, she was unable to because of her illness.

Janie and Amy would rush to Auntie Margie. "Read us a story! Look at this drawing! Let's play a game!" Every photograph shows Margie in the center, Janie on one side, Amy on the other. They hugged their Auntie Margie tight like a sandwich. Margie's gift of gab and storytelling abilities kept my daughters silly and laughing and asking for more.

I maintain a vision of Margie at thirty-three, two years before she died. Margie sits on the floor reading to my two daughters. Janie gazes up at her with loving eyes. Amy bends her head, proudly showing Margie the bow in her hair. Margie's big heart is on display—putting my girls first and enjoying the time with her nieces. The love is evident in their smiles.

1963 - Judy 7, Jane 4, Margie 9.

1958 - Judy 2, Margie 4.

1964 - Margie 10, Judy 8, Jane 5.

1965 - Judy 9, Jane 6.

1965 - Judy 9, Margie 11.

1966 - Margie 12, Jane 7.

1968 - Margie 14.

1970 - Jane 11.

1979 - Judy 23, Jane 20.

1980 - Margie 26, Jane 21, Judy 24.

1981 - Jane 21.

1984 - Margie 30.

2015 - Celebration of Sisters.

2018 - Judy, Celebraton of Sisters.

Margie 10, Judy 8, Jane 5.

Finale - Celebration of Sisters

Finale - Celebration of Sisters

1962 - Margie 8, Judy 6.

CHAPTER 8

Tides Are Changing

MEMORY: THE BUZZER RANG—IT WAS TIME FOR THE SESSION TO START. WE RACED TO GET ONTO THE ICE AT BOSTON COLLEGE, EXCITED TO SKATE, ALL DRESSED UP IN SKATING DRESSES AND WARM GLOVES. MARGIE STEPPED ONTO THE ICE FIRST, JANE SECOND, AND I, A BIT TENTATIVELY HOLDING ONTO THE BOARDS, THIRD.

Grief can't stay hidden forever. My grief was hiding deep in my subconscious, and over the years, it would come bubbling up to the surface at the most random times. One of those times was on a warm September day in 1990, a month after Margie died. I was sitting with a friend waiting to pick up our daughters from elementary school. Two of Margie's old classmates passed on the walkway heading into the building. One had been a cheerleader with Margie, and they'd spent many summers at camp together. The other pointed and whispered, but she spoke loudly enough for me to hear.

"That's Margie Lipson's sister," she said. "Margie's the one who died of mental illness."

I sat on the bench paralyzed, mute. I wish I had been able to say something, to talk with them about Margie, my beautiful, caring sister.

Six months after Margie died, I was clearly experiencing

grief but without knowing the full extent of it all. So on a cold winter night, my parents dragged me to a meeting with the Compassionate Friends, a nonprofit organization that provided hope and support for people who were grieving. Their focus was mostly on parents grieving over the loss of a child, but they also offered support for the loss of a sibling. My parents assembled with others in the large meeting room while I went off to the smaller room with other siblings, one as young as thirteen, and I was the oldest at thirty-three. Gray metal chairs were planted in a circle, and introductions were made.

"Hi, I'm Andy. I lost my twelve-year-old brother Stephen after an eight-year battle with leukemia."

"Hi, I'm Sarah. I lost my brother Joe, eighteen, in a car accident."

"I'm Anne Marie. I found my twenty-year-old sister Joanne in a pool of blood. She was murdered."

Hearing these stories only escalated my pain—the deaths were too fresh, overwhelming, daunting. And being the only one who had lost *two* siblings made me feel different, separate, and alone. My thoughts wandered and I became disengaged. It was too soon for me to realize that I did, in fact, have commonalities with these mourning siblings. I felt such a jumble of feelings but could not verbalize them to anyone. I could not comprehend how much I did, in fact, need the group or should have reached out to one individual on the telephone. Unable to embrace the warmth and support of the group, I did not return.

In retrospect, had I been patient and made a connection with at least one other individual from the supportive group, perhaps I would not have felt so alone for years. At the time, I did not realize the impact of not only the losses of both my sisters layered with having Margie's illness weighing on the family for twenty years. Afraid to be open and share my feelings, I ran away.

From that point, I took what I now call the "fast track"—racing through each of the daily tasks related to working and raising two daughters alone and being there for my parents—and I actively avoided talking about grief or acknowledging my sadness as being the sole surviving Lipson daughter.

After my daughters were born, my parents and I spoke on the phone daily. Their sole focus in life was me and my daughters and watching Jane and Amy grow up. I was grateful for their help and the girls adored their Grandma and Papa.

"Judy, you sound tired," my father said one Sunday night on the phone.

"Daddy, it's just my usual Sunday—preparing for the week, cooking meals, loading up backpacks, and getting organized." The next night after work, the doorbell rang. My father stood there, his arms loaded with shopping bags filled with prepared dinners, enough to load the freezer for weeks.

Every Friday, I picked up my daughters from school, gave them a snack in the car, and drove them to group lessons at the same rink at Boston College where my sisters and I had ice-skated. I sat in the stands and watched Janie and Amy fall and get up, and fall and get up as they learned to skate. A warmth flowed through me. This was a tradition passed down, a thread connecting my sisters to my daughters.

One Friday as the lessons finished, I bumped into one of Jane's friends, Meri. Immediately, my eyes welled up. I had not seen her in many years. Both she and her sister had gone to camp with Jane and me. We shared a brief hug and hello. My hands trembled as I helped my girls off with their skates into their sneakers.

I ran into Meri a few more times because we both lived in the same town. She relayed memories that made me smile.

"Me and Jane used to go through your room when we were young girls. After we rummaged through your belongings, Jane insisted everything must be put back in its exact spot," she said.

I found this endearing, as Jane had often seemed ashamed of me. I was never "cool" enough for her or her friends. For the weekend of Jane's sixteenth birthday, I made a special trip home from college to join in her celebration. Yet, I was banished to the kitchen and not allowed to participate in any of the festivities. Jane's friends did not acknowledge me. I felt shunned and extremely hurt. Jane and I had many sisterly fights when she was a teenager, but I suppose that is what teenagers do.

Meri's husband had dated Jane, and he had also lost a brother. He and I ran into each other, too, and we talked about Jane and losing a sibling. To be able to face Jane's friends—and not run away—was a huge hurdle to overcome. But I did. Seeing Jane's friends had eventually become bearable, though a part of me would always feel sad, bittersweet, like a piece of very dark chocolate.

I was still conflicted about my emotions but I did not run from them. After both of my sisters died, I felt an obligation to accompany my father to the annual memorial Yizkor service on Yom Kippur. *How can my poor father stand and recite the Mourner's Prayer for two deceased daughters all alone?* I thought. Though I dreaded the service, I never slowed my thinking down long enough to ask, *What do I want?* Or to admit, *I am just not emotionally capable of attending this service.* Seeing Margie's and Jane's names in the memorial book hit me hard.

After Margie died, my anxiety would escalate and my emotions would flood with waves of tears in the weeks before Yom Kippur. Inside the synagogue, anticipating the Mourner's

Prayer, my body would tremble from head to toe until it was racked by shaking sobs. When the rabbi asked us to stand, I stood with my head down, blowing my nose, blinded by tears. My father placed his arm around my shoulder. By the end of the prayer, I felt unsteady and my vision blurred by tears, but I managed to walk out of the temple. I was emotionally and physically depleted, and I gracefully declined invitations to join others to break the fast. All I could face was to go home, rid myself of my pantyhose, dress, and high heels, throw on sweatpants and a sweatshirt, and do absolutely nothing. I was nothing more than a dishrag. After many years of forcing this "obligation" upon myself, I finally recognized the damage it was causing. *No more,* I thought, and made the choice not to go the following year.

But in 2000, almost twenty years after the deaths of my sisters, I believe my grief recovery started, though I didn't know it at the time. A routine physical exam revealed a lump in my right breast. I was referred to a breast surgeon, who in a matter-of-fact demeanor relayed the plan of a needle biopsy, and if necessary, surgical removal of the lump.

I sat on the examining table in a medical gown and cried. The nurse took my hands in hers, looked directly into my eyes, and tried to comfort me. I blurted out that I had lost both sisters. I said the words out loud that had been dormant on my mind and lips for years. Perhaps it was a trickle of Margie and Jane bubbling to the surface. But that wasn't the case after all. They crept down to my subconscious for another ten years.

Thoughts circled through my head. *Could this actually be happening? Could one family possibly lose all three daughters?*

The lump had to be removed. On the morning of the procedure, I conducted the business as usual of a single mother working full time. My oldest daughter was a freshman in high school. My younger daughter was in middle school. I dressed in my usual work clothes and drove my daughters to school so as not to worry them or disrupt their regular routine. My mother accompanied me to the hospital.

My father picked up my daughters at school and calmly told them I was undergoing a procedure. Unfortunately, because I'd created a ruse in the morning, my poor father was forced to explain a delicate situation to my daughters, which he did quite well. "Papa" was their rock, so if he said their mother would be fine, they believed him.

I sweated out the week until the test results arrived. The lump was benign. I survived. My family did not have to live through another tragedy. Looking back, I realized how important that moment was for me to voice my grief to a stranger, a glimpse of a moment igniting the spark of my recovery. To put those words out into the air, to say out loud that my sisters were gone.

CHAPTER 9

Why Now?

MEMORY: WITH MY BIRTHDAY IN OCTOBER, I WAS EXCITED TO FINALLY TAKE MY DRIVING TEST. MOST OF MY FRIENDS ALREADY HAD THEIR LICENSES. MY MOTHER SAT IN THE BACK SEAT. I WAITED. "JUDY, GO," SHE SAID. THE INSTRUCTOR TURNED TO MY MOTHER AND SAID, "MA'AM, IF YOU ARE NOT QUIET, WE WILL HAVE TO ASK YOU TO LEAVE."

There is no recipe for grief.

Over thirty years my grief hit peaks and valleys. Much as one twin might feel a loss of symmetry without the other, I continuously felt like my own symmetry was off, like a part of me was missing. The night Jane died, both Margie and I woke up in the middle of the night at the exact moment of her death. Although Margie and I never spoke about Jane's death, several years later, we had a telephone conversation:

"Judy, I watched *Mary Tyler Moore* and I thought of you, Bren."

"Thanks, Rho, I miss you."

"I miss you too. Can I tell you something?"

"Sure."

"The night Jane died I bolted up at three a.m."

"Oh my God, so did I. That is so weird."

That's all we said, she abruptly changed the subject back

to the rerun of the show. We joked about how similar we were to the characters on *The Mary Tyler Moore Show*—Margie paralleled Rhoda and I paralleled Brenda. Rhoda represented the confident, married, older sister, and Brenda, the single sister, not as confident. I called Margie "Rho," and she called me "Bren."

Margie and I never discussed Jane or her death again.

When Margie died, I knew her death was imminent, yet it was still a shock. But Jane's death always haunted me. A few years after Margie died, I needed to find the answers to Jane's accident. My parents had kept secrets, thinking I was not strong enough to handle the truth. Their secrets had only elevated my fear.

I suspected the real truth had been kept from me. My parents told me Jane's car malfunctioned, but that did not ring true. Jane was gone, nothing would change that, but after Margie died, I just needed to know.

I made a call to the local police to obtain a copy of the records. I did not tell a soul.

It was a Thursday at ten in the morning. Surprised by my calmness, I walked into the station escorted into a room by a police officer. Like a scene from a movie, I sat down on a metal chair at a desk in a dank, gray room. The officer sat across from me, his hands crossed on the manila folder. I started to shake.

Blinded by tears, I read the report. Due to speed, Jane had lost control, hit a tree, and died on impact. Seeing her name on the report—Jane Lipson, female, age twenty-two, deceased— her death felt real. A young man in the car had survived, but his name was not on the report. Now I knew the truth. I blocked it out of my mind for the next fifteen years.

Then in 2010, it seemed like the universe was trying to tell me something. In temple one Saturday, Margie's friend Barbara asked if we could meet. I said I'd get back to her. *Why did she want to talk to me? Why now?* My knee-jerk reaction was to keep my guard up and decline. But after thinking about it, I changed my mind. My Margie had been ill for twenty years and was now gone for twenty years. How astounding that a friend was still thinking about her!

We met for coffee and sat down to catch up. I finally asked in a soft voice, "What about Margie?"

Barbara took a deep breath, then said, "I think about her all the time. When I was in high school, Margie dragged me to a Jewish fair where I made a connection that changed my life." This ultimately led her toward a rewarding career in Jewish philanthropy that she had enjoyed for thirty years. "It gave me direction and purpose," she continued, "and without Margie I would not be where I am today." She wanted me to know what an impact Margie had had on her life.

Margie had such a generous spirit, but her eating disorder dominated her life so much that we sometimes lost sight of it. How grateful I felt to listen to her friend's heartfelt story! How wonderful to know that, despite all her pain and suffering, Margie had changed someone's life.

I sat in my car for a few minutes after coffee with Barbara. Happy memories of Margie flooded my mind. I closed my eyes and thought about the Big Sister rules. This was the unwritten code in my relationship with Margie. "Come on, Lipson," she'd say with her big-brown-eyes look, and I never refused. That was her favorite phrase, and she would say it before any type of request, which usually wasn't ever a real request.

"Come on, Lipson, let's rearrange my room," Margie would say. *Oh no, here we go again*, I would think. First, we'd move the bed with the pink bedspread and pink afghan, crocheted by Gram, to the opposite wall. Then the desk and chair with the pink cushion went under the window. And finally, we'd push the heaviest dresser to the wall closest to the door.

"Thanks, Lipson, I love it," Margie would say, only to move it all back a week later.

The guitar in the corner next to the closet never got moved. When Margie first got the guitar, she played it well and learned some chords. I lasted about a minute, so I switched to piano. Margie continued to sing and play guitar beautifully. We played duets together, and the guitar went everywhere with Margie. She also loved listening to music. She had a record player on a little table in her room, and she played her favorite 33s by Diana Ross, James Taylor, Carole King, and Steven Stills.

One day Margie had three friends over to practice for the musical, *You're a Good Man, Charlie Brown.* Usually, they huddled together in Margie's room, but they asked me to play the piano in the living room while they sang the song. I could barely hide my elation. Directed by Margie, I sat on the needlepoint bench playing the baby grand piano, looking at the four of them as they danced and bellowed at the top of their lungs, "What a good man you are . . ." I felt like I had been given the keys to the kingdom.

That meeting with Barbara helped put me on a trajectory of healing. I was finally able to talk about my sister to someone who knew her. For thirty years I not only buried my grief, but I also buried memories of my sisters. I didn't talk about them to anyone—family or friends. After that meeting with Barbara, I realized how much I needed to talk about my sisters, how deeply I missed Margie and Jane.

A few months later, I ran into Jane's friend Lisa, whom I had not seen since Jane's death. I asked her to meet me for coffee. Some of Jane's friends had intimidated me in my youth, but we were adults and had changed.

Lisa adored Jane. We reminisced how they sneaked into my room to "borrow" some of my clothes, giggling. Why would Jane want to borrow my clothes in the first place? Jane had sprayed perfume to mask the smell of cigarettes. As if I didn't know. I remember throwing the sweater back at her, insisting she clean it. What did she think I was, stupid? Lisa and I had a good laugh.

Our conversation turned serious as Lisa relayed Jane's words on the night before she died. It was Jane's twenty-second birthday, and her parting words came in the form of a toast. "I do not have a job or a home," Jane said. "But I have lots of friends."

Jane's friend promised to keep in touch, but she didn't keep that promise. Perhaps seeing me was too painful.

I got into my car, teary-eyed with thoughts of Jane. So many what-ifs. What happened to the precious little girl with the blonde hair who stood by my side? Why didn't she believe in herself?

Jane loved working with small children, as is reflected in one of my favorite black-and-white photos of Jane gazing down at a child in her lap. Jane and the child are smiling, and Jane is actually beaming. In middle and high school, Jane worked as a student aide in a combined kindergarten-first grade classroom, helping with creative projects and correcting students' workbooks and papers. Jane excelled at this, and she enjoyed working with children. Her supervisors gave her glowing recommendations based on the great work she did. Spending time with children provided Jane a sense of comfort, reward, and accomplishment. That was Jane's happy place.

Jane had a gift and would have been an amazing preschool teacher. But she did not have enough self-esteem or direction to follow through. She lacked concentration and focus and was distracted by socialization and parties. Jane's continued partying and lack of focus left her with no choice but to move home after college. With most of her friends at various colleges, Jane worked in retail and took a few courses at a local college in Boston, still uncertain about a career. She was frustrated and miserable living at home.

I was shocked and saddened to hear what Jane had said about herself on the night of her birthday. If only she could have known how special she was. Still, hearing that Jane remained in the minds and hearts of her friends provided me comfort.

I always wonder how my life could have changed if only I had opened up a bit sooner. After meeting with Barbara and Lisa, something stirred in me. It was if I was standing on the precipice of an awakening of sorts, but I teetered there. I wasn't ready to take the leap into my full healing . . . at least not yet.

For years I had isolated myself. I'd avoided taking any actions that might have contributed to my growth, comfort, identity—always afraid. When I did open the door, Margie and Jane's friends embraced me and shared their stories of my sisters. They had patiently waited years for me to come around.

CHAPTER 10

Thirty-Year Milestone

MEMORY: WE SIT AROUND THE DINING TABLE ON PINS AND NEEDLES WAITING TO OPEN OUR CHANUKAH PRESENTS PILED UP AT OUR ASSIGNED SEATS—ONE PERSON, ONE PRESENT AT A TIME. JANE SQUEALS IN DELIGHT AT THE SUSIE Q DOLL, MARGIE IS EXCITED WITH HER PASTELS, AND I PEEL BACK THE WRAPPING TO REVEAL MY GIFT—THE CLASSIC DICE GAME, YAHTZEE.

The swift passage of years from 1981 to 2011 reminded me of Paragon Park, the amusement park Jane and I visited as children before we went to camp. The roller coaster would fly down the tracks at high speed, then suddenly slow and creep upward, inch by inch. *Just like life.*

Every amusement ride demonstrated the same changes we experience as humans every day—in energy, power, stamina, speed, fear, thrills, and anguish—from the excitement created by the music as the hand-painted horses of the merry-go-round began to glide up and down, to the thrill of completing a ride and the anticipation of wanting to go back again and again, to the disappointment, even torment, of failing to win a game or prize.

Throughout the years, I attempted therapy and had some good outcomes, but nothing that really helped push me forward and deal with my grief head-on. That doesn't mean I didn't get anything out of therapy in those years. Quite the contrary. But everything changed in 2011. My therapist at the time did not push but encouraged me to pursue grief therapy. Thus began the initial dialogue about Margie and Jane.

The year of 2011 was a milestone year. It was the thirty-year anniversary of Jane's passing, I turned fifty-five, my father passed away, and I moved to downtown Boston. That was also the year of the inauguration of Celebration of Sisters.

Even at the beginning, my grief work made me feel like I was at the amusement park with my entire family reliving the ups and downs, glittery gaiety and blandness, noise and quiet, anticipation and setbacks—but most of all, the glory of those precious times we all spent together and what they revealed.

Working with the therapist on grief and being more open about Margie and Jane made me realize I needed to find a venue to pay tribute to my sisters. Philanthropy was a staple in our family. We always volunteered for various organizations and donated where we could. The Marjorie E. and Jane E. Lipson Memorial Fund was established in 1999 at Massachusetts General Hospital due to the exemplary care Margie received at the early onset of her tragic illness.

One day, a friend and I met for lunch. A philanthropist herself, I broached the idea of establishing a fundraiser for Margie and Jane.

"What would be the best way to honor your sisters?" she asked.

We bantered back and forth. I did not want a traditional fundraiser—a boring dinner or the typical golf tournament. A breast cancer survivor, she suggested a 5K run or walk. We jotted down notes. What would be the most meaningful way to honor Margie and Jane? What did we all have in common?

I decided that ice-skating was the perfect choice. We had all skated as girls. Sponsoring an ice-skating event would be unique and fun and meaningful as it would provide a real connection to my sisters and their heritage. My sisters' birthdays were in November, so we scheduled the ice-skating event for the first weekend in November. We called it the Celebration of Sisters.

We needed a master of ceremonies. Mark, a friend of Margie's, offered to meet and talk. I was just starting to step out of my "guard is always up" zone and had begun meeting new people, reaching out, and talking about my sisters. But I was ready. Mark and I agreed to meet at Panera Bread for coffee.

It was a hot, sunny day as I pulled into the parking lot. I sat in the car for a moment, taking deep breaths and trying to calm down. I was nervous. I had a vague recollection of Mark in Margie's large circle of friends, none of whom ever paid attention to me.

I headed inside and found Mark sitting at a corner table near the window. Mark's soft demeanor instantly put me at ease. He shared his experience fundraising for pediatric cancer. The gleam in his eye showed his passion. "How can I help you?" he asked. "What do you need?" We talked more about Celebration of Sisters and updates on various classmates. I told him a funny story about one of his classmates—a "smelly boy"—and we had a good laugh.

When we were younger, my parents sent my sisters and me to Hebrew school three days a week. Our carpools were shared with two older boys whom we labeled the "smelly boys" because of their awful cologne. The three of us would race out of school to claim the front seat. The poor girl who finished last got stuck in the back seat with the smelly boys. I suspect most times I ended up in the back.

Mark confessed a crush on Margie, though they'd never

dated. He invited me to their fortieth high school reunion. He said he would ask Margie's classmates to be sponsors and attend Celebration of Sisters.

I felt warmed by his kindness and generosity, but I also felt the hole in my heart—the ache that panged and throbbed whenever my mind jumped to what my sisters were missing, like how sad it was that Margie couldn't attend the reunion herself.

A few weeks later, as I drove to Margie's reunion, my body wouldn't stop shaking. That should have been a red flag warning me to immediately turn around. When I pulled into the parking lot, I quickly found a spot and sat there for a long time, taking deep breaths to try to calm myself. After getting enough courage, I went inside. The black-and-white photo of Margie on the memorial table set me off. There she was, my beautiful Margie, her smile, the sparkle in her eyes, and her long, silky brown hair.

I chatted with a few people from our original neighborhood.

One of Margie's classmates, a photographer who grew up a few blocks from us and whose father was our plumber, had not changed a bit. We exchanged pleasantries about our families, but the conversation felt a bit strained. *Why wouldn't it be?* There was an elephant in the room, and it was Margie—of whom we made no mention. A few others hugged me. One remembered riding bicycles with Margie. How much I had wanted to connect with Margie's friends, but the introduction of so many people at once felt overwhelming, and with great emotion, I left.

I do remember beating myself up for not staying, but something had changed in me. I had given myself permission to feel proud about going to such an event. The fact that I was able to recognize and congratulate myself for doing something that I knew was going to make me uncomfortable was a big step in the right direction. It was the first time I'd felt hopeful that I would be able to approach my grief in a new way.

In the winter of 2011, I made the momentous decision to move to downtown Boston, and I actually moved in August. A life in the city could help me reclaim the excitement I'd enjoyed in New York in my twenties. I loved the hustle and bustle right outside my door, the freedom to walk everywhere. Having everything I needed a stone's throw away—groceries, shopping, theaters, music, museums, sports, restaurants, and public transit—made me feel alive.

Downsizing from a house to an apartment was tough. Some storage boxes had been untouched for nineteen years. A discolored yellow box contained birthday cards, notes, and letters from Margie and Jane. I pulled out one piece at a time. The box remained in the corner, and every day I grabbed a few. Margie and I had fostered a mutual admiration society.

"I love you very much and you mean the world to me."

"I love you dearly and cherish you."

"I truly treasure our relationship and feel we are so lucky to be as close as we are."

"We can always talk and understand each other."

The cards Jane sent expressed that, no matter what, we were sisters and would always be there for each other. Jane had faith in me. I hope she knew that I had faith in her. I read her words over and over.

When I sat with my daughters, who were twenty-five and twenty-six at the time, and explained my decision to sell their childhood home, neither was happy. In fact, both were quite angry.

"This is our home," they said. "Where will we go?"

"We've had nineteen years of memories—holidays, birthday parties, first days of school, proms, going off to college, trick or treating, and Shabbat dinners in this home. No one is going to take that away," I said. "But you both have your own apartments now."

The timing of this decision coincided with the steep decline of my father's health; I think it felt like a double loss in their eyes. From my own perspective, I was not abandoning my daughters; I needed to forge ahead.

What really helped me have some clarity was when my parents generously sent me to the Dorothy Hamill Adult Figure Skating Fantasy Camp in Nantucket, Massachusetts, for my fifty-fifth birthday. This event was spectacular, but it also came with some sadness. This was just months before my father died. I saw him the day before camp started, and he looked sicker than I had ever seen him. I left for camp with a heavy heart.

For five days on the gorgeous island of Nantucket, twenty-five adult skaters stayed at an inn right off the main street. A van shuttled us back and forth to the rink. Every morning we gathered in a circle to warm up with the theme of the day—joy, happiness, peace, serenity, and love. Then we skated for several hours among the kind, supportive coaches who had competed in the Olympics or world or national championships. During lunch, in the warm summer sunshine, we exchanged our life and skating stories. We did not care that we had blisters on our feet. In the afternoons, we learned the choreography for our final performance. Our stunning itinerary included dinners and sights on Nantucket.

Is this real? I thought one day, as Randy Gardner, a figure skating Olympian, took several laps around the rink with me. *Am I dreaming?* His arm was positioned around my waist as we stroked together, crossing one foot over the other and circling the corners of the rink.

Tim Murphy, a master of skating choreography—the only choreographer Dorothy Hamill used for her solos—choreographed two numbers for us to perform in a show for the Nantucket community. The song, "When You Wish Upon a Star," felt like magic. I had never been in an ice show. That skating performance brought up so many images and emotions. I thought about skating with Margie and Jane, my father at death's door, my feeling of freedom on the ice, and my finally being able to release myself to the presence of joy. My two daughters came to see me skate. I was elated to be on the ice and to revel in this exciting moment with them by my side.

Ice-skating camp had been life changing. It was a new and fabulous experience to be accepted into this new community that was so warm, welcoming, and encouraging. I had not thought it possible to meet other adult skaters who would open so many doors and new opportunities. Attending the camp was the first time I'd stepped out of my comfort zone for myself, on my own. It had felt like a fantasy but turned out to be a gift.

The very first Celebration of Sisters was scheduled for November 3. I needed to choose the photographs for the premier of Celebration of Sisters. I sifted through boxes of photos and recalled precious memories of the three of us feeding the pigeons in the Boston Common, or taking a swim in the pool at a resort in Maine.

Then I found it, the perfect photo! It was a black-and-white of the Lipson sisters sitting on a slide in our backyard. We were squished together, oldest to youngest, Margie at the top, Jane at the bottom, her chubby hands grasping the sides of the slide tightly, and me in the middle. Margie and Jane wore sleeveless tops, shorts, and flip-flops. As the middle sister being independent and different, I wore a different outfit from my sisters—a short-sleeve top, shorts, and sneakers, and I was wearing a watch.

When my father died on October 27, I had a difficult decision to make. *Should I cancel the event?* The decline of my father's health for seven years and his death hit me hard. My father, Benjamin Lipson, had been the patriarch and mentor of our family, dispensing guidance with a larger-than-life personality.

Though my family wanted me to cancel, a voice in my head kept repeating that we should forge ahead. Delaying or canceling the event would cause us to lose our momentum. This was the inception of the fundraiser—we'd publicized it, and all of the preparations were in place. Everything and everyone was ready. With the same push-and-pull emotions I'd felt in the past, I decided that the event must go on. I'm not sure whether my mother and daughters ever forgave me for holding the event so close to my father's death. But I felt I had no choice.

The initial Celebration of Sisters event was held at the Hampshire House in Boston, with a cocktail party featuring a live trio. There was a PowerPoint presentation of the Lipson sisters with speeches from a representative from Massachusetts General Hospital and myself. Dolled up in a purple dress, I delivered my remarks with a shaky voice. There was so much love and support in the room, not only for my sisters, but the realization that my family had just endured another loss. The following year commenced the ice-skating, our signature event.

Celebration of Sisters was the one thing that truly helped me heal from decades of grief that caused horrific pain and anxiety, which exponentially intensified in the month of November around my sisters' birthdays. Like a miracle, Celebration of Sisters alleviated some of that anguish. It changed the focus from Margie's and Jane's deaths to the joy of celebrating their lives. With the added weight of mourning for my father just before the initial Celebration, I don't think I could have survived if we'd canceled.

Celebration of Sisters was mine. It was something I had created to commemorate my sisters and channel my grief. It gave me a voice.

CHAPTER 11

Circles of Comfort

MEMORY: ON A FAMILY VACATION TO MIAMI IN THE 1960S, JANE AND I BOUNCED ON THE TRAMPOLINE ADJACENT TO THE POOL THAT WAS OVERLOOKING THE OCEAN. HOLDING HANDS, WE FACED EACH OTHER AND SQUEALED AS WE JUMPED UP AND DOWN.

After the first Celebration of Sisters event in 2011, I felt like a heaviness had been lifted. I was grieving, but I never realized how heavy grief could physically feel, how painful and sharp it can cut, like a blade on a smooth ice surface.

My skating had given me momentum—forward and backward, side to side. There were times when my grief would hit me with no warning. Standing in line at the grocery store and someone's laugh reminded me of Jane. Hearing a song on the radio that reminded me of Margie. I would bite back tears, or let them fall, or whisper "I love you" under my breath. And then I would go about whatever I was doing, moving on and moving forward.

The Celebration of Sisters ice-skating fundraising event in November 2012 was a special thing that really guided me to the path of healing. I had always envisioned for it be an ice-skating event, and that finally came to fruition. It was held in a small ice rink with one set of bleachers and ten skaters. I chose to skate to Whitney Houston's "I Will Always Love You." My body shook as I performed with my partner, holding on tight. After the finale, as the skaters lapped around the rink and waved to the crowd, I stopped to hug my mother and daughters. We celebrated Margie and Jane, bringing them forward. Sharing them finally brought me out of the darkness and into the light.

I had made a huge breakthrough. For decades, I couldn't even talk about my sisters. Now, the stories of Margie, Judy, and Jane were out there for the masses. My attempt to heal from the grief and loss was channeled through the joy of my childhood pastime of ice-skating. There was no turning back, but I didn't want to. I couldn't wait to plan the next fundraising event—it gave me a purpose and a path to healing that I hadn't even thought possible.

In 2013, I received an incredible gift. A cousin gave me a video of Margie she'd kept all these years. Excited to see my sister, I took a deep breath and clicked Play. On the video, Margie was having dinner at our grandmother's house. She was directing Gram on where to place the dishes. Gram's table was adorned with her fine china, chicken salad with grapes, cranberry Jell-O mold, and her specially baked molasses and sugar cookies. Margie was seated at the table, her brittle hair pulled back in a limp ponytail, her deeply pronounced high cheekbones, and brown eyes lined with her signature black eyeliner.

Tears streamed down my face. Seeing Margie in movement . . . it felt like only yesterday but also like a century ago. It was Margie's voice, Margie's tiny body. I conjured up an image of Margie, the vivacious cheerleader bouncing up and down with green-and-white pom-poms on the middle school football field. All smiles, bubbly green skirt, white sweater with the M for Meadowbrook, white sneakers and socks, rosy red cheeks, surrounded by fellow cheerleaders laughing. Then I focused on Margie on the video. *My sister is so beautiful*, I thought.

I watched the video over and over. The clip was only thirty seconds, but for me, an eternity. My Margie, her voice. Surprised and relieved, I was able to recall what Margie's voice had sounded like when we had hung out in her pink bedroom.

"Lipson, put on Diana Ross—let's dance."

Although not a fan of social media, it was a tool to reconnect with family and friends. With only a few Lipson cousins remaining, I reached out to a cousin who lived in the area. Two years went by before I received a Facebook message. Immediately, I emailed her and we reconnected.

I had not seen this cousin since I was sixteen at Jane's bat mitzvah in March 1973. Yet, we both felt an instant connection, an immediate closeness, comfort, safety, and trust that enabled me to divulge my deepest, most precious thoughts. Our lives paralleled with losses, secrets, and pressures. She had recently lost her brother.

Her family had lived in a big, old house in Connecticut, and when we visited during my childhood, we played outside walking on stilts. I'd loved her magnificent wooden dollhouse with its intricate furniture. The dollhouse moved through many houses and thankfully was in her home the day I visited. She had invited me over for lunch so I could reconnect with her— and the dollhouse. When I saw the little rooms with the tiny furniture still intact, I could hardly believe it. I felt so uplifted that I had rekindled a bond with a family member who still thought fondly of Margie and Jane.

Despite decades apart, my cousin and I were never at a loss for words. We shared memories of our fathers who were very close first cousins. My father worked in the insurance business with her grandfather. I gave her a paperweight that had been her grandfather's I'd discovered when I cleaned out my father's office. We exchanged old family photos. With all that we both had lost, finding each other felt like coming home.

Reconnecting with people from my past continued in the months that followed. Friends from my past were a thread to Margie and Jane in addition to me. We had history. They knew me and my sisters. No explanations needed. It felt like coming home, safe, secure. Whether I chose to talk about Margie or Jane, I knew the door was always open, and after thirty years I gave myself permission and the ability to do so.

Some of my old classmates circled around to support Celebration of Sisters. My childhood friend Debbie attended the ice-skating event year after year. I remember she had enjoyed a trip to Florida with the Lipson sisters in 1965.

Oh, how I miss traveling together as a family! My mother was an expert at planning all the trips. She planned the family vacation to the Beau Rivage in Miami, Florida, in 1965. She liked to dress us up in matching outfits. That year, she outfitted us from head to toe with matching clothing: bathing suits, white terry cloth cover-ups, shorts sets, socks with lace, and pretty summer dresses from a very nice children's shop in Waban, Massachusetts, opposite the T stop. Our mother had a lot of patience with three girls ages eleven, nine, and six, all of multiple sizes running in different directions in the store. Three sisters dressed in matching outfits, and Jane—the recipient of the hand-me-downs—wore the same clothing for many years. I remember the weather that year in Florida was dismal. It rained five of the seven days of our vacation. Without the warm sun, pool, and beach, our activities were limited. The hotel provided a few games. We sulked in the hotel lobby. Many of the beautiful getups my mother enjoyed buying for us did not get worn.

In the summer of 2013, Debbie and I met regularly and ice-skated together like we did as young girls. I found I could talk freely with old friends or acquaintances who had known my sisters. Now we could talk about anything—our parents, motherhood, life.

I even reconnected with friends from elementary school. Robert, a friend from my childhood, sent a me a message on Facebook saying that he'd thought I was sweet in school and thought I would do great things in life. I was astounded when he said he followed the posts from Celebration of Sisters. Some days it had all felt so obscure, but it was becoming clear to me that people were actually out there following our efforts, becoming more aware of sibling loss and grief. Nothing could have felt more rewarding; it has helped me heal.

Someone once said to me, "Jane gave you life for twenty-two years, and Margie gave you life for thirty-five years. Some people never experience having a sister at all." That gave me a whole new way of appreciating what I'd had, and it helped me find light and comfort rather than falling into darker thoughts.

CHAPTER 12

Complicated Grief

MEMORY: "I'LL GIVE YOU A CHARLESTON CHEW FOR
MILK DUDS, OKAY?" SAID MARGIE TO JANE. "HOW ABOUT
JUJYFRUITS FOR SUGAR DADDY?" I ASKED MARGIE, AS THE
THREE OF US SORTED OUR ABUNDANCE OF HALLOWEEN
CANDY IN THE DINING ROOM.

I had been unalterably damaged by the deaths of my sisters,
even broken. Day after day, month after month, and year after
year had turned into decade after decade marking my disabling
inability to grieve. I needed help.

In 2016, I became truly fortunate to be accepted into a
complicated grief study at Massachusetts General Hospital in
Boston. *Complicated grief* is defined as a prolonged grief disorder
persisting after the death of a loved one(s). Symptoms can
include disbelief that the deaths occurred, difficulty sleeping,
guilt, avoidance, lack of motivation, feelings of unworthiness,
post-traumatic reactions, difficulties in close relationships, and
trust issues. I met numerous criteria.

The study required five excruciating months of intense
weekly one-on-one therapy sessions, cognitive behavioral
therapy, and homework assignments that sent me to severely
dark spaces. It provided a parallel focus on restoring myself.
I had a constant daily accountability requirement of rating

my feelings when performing tasks like looking at pictures of my sisters, trying to recall the actual deaths of my sisters, and listening to recorded sessions in which I described the harrowing details of the deaths of my sisters. In contrast, the study also required me to carve out time for myself, for the first time in decades, and engage in activities that provided restoration and joy.

I tried a few more Compassionate Friends sibling meetings in Boston. I felt more open-minded, a bit more willing to listen and accept help, and many of the comments and handouts resonated. Interactions with several members continued outside of the meetings. I met a bereaved sibling who shared with me his experience about participation in a complicated grief program. That was what spurred the idea for me to continue my work on grief and apply to the complicated grief study.

A criterion of the study required sharing the experience with family and friends. I started with my daughters. As my daughters grew up, our home was full of love and warmth. We had structure and rules, but always lots of laughter and fun.

One Sunday afternoon I visited my younger daughter, Amy, in her apartment. We sat on the couch facing each other. I explained that because I had never processed my grief after my sisters died, I had been accepted into a complicated grief study, and I hoped it would help me. As an extremely private person, sharing this was a huge stepping out of the box for me.

I would never forget what Amy said to me that day. "Grief defines you." Her words hurt me to the core. I burst into tears. As a mother, I had tried so hard to hide my sorrow. After I told my older daughter, Janie, of my participation in the study, she, too, admitted that she had detected a sadness in me, and she encouraged me to do whatever I had to do.

I wondered if my daughters had sensed a shift in me after

my father died in 2011. That was when I realized for the first time I needed to start the process of truly grieving. Before 2011, I felt I'd been there for my daughters 24/7, but after my father's passing, I'd started to take steps to care for myself. More importantly, I realized that caring for myself was not a selfish thing to do but rather a healthy thing. Still, they saw a mother who had changed.

As our family's plans for the Passover holiday took shape— in the middle of my complicated grief study—it became hard to go along with everyone's wishes and expectations as usual. And it was an exceptional strain for my daughters to witness my pain.

"Girls, this year, how about we have the holiday together, just us," I said. "I'm not up to chitchatting with a crowd. Participating in this study and Grandma's move have taken too much out of me."

"We really want to go to Lexington and be with the Miller clan," my daughters said. "It's a tradition."

"If you feel you want to go, you go. But I'm going to pass." I stuck to my guns.

"Mommy, we really want you to come," they pleaded.

But making small talk and being all smiles was just too arduous. So I didn't go. It was my choice. My family went without me.

During the study, what my daughters missed most was the laughter. I tried so hard to be upbeat. I'd always said I would make a terrible poker player. My face could not mask my emotions. My daughters yearned to hear stories of their aunts Margie and Jane that I had deprived them of. Little by little, I started to introduce them to their aunts. I so often see traces of my sisters in my daughters.

The study required my careful attention to documentation.

Day one, I was handed a white notebook. "That's for your notes," the therapist said. "Place the most important documents in the front pocket."

Because of the intensity of the therapy, I was required to make a plan in case I needed help between sessions. *Who could I call?* This meant sharing that I was enrolled in a complicated grief study. *This is not a secret,* I reminded myself. It was the essential help I needed for my grief journey. I was learning to break old patterns.

Nervously, I called my friend. "Lisa . . ." I stuttered, choking back tears.

"I'm so proud of you," she said after I shared my need for support. "This must be really hard. With all that I know about you, we never discussed Margie and Jane, and now I hope we can. You know I am always here for you." *Phew,* relieved, touched, and step one accomplished.

On that first day, I cried through the entire hour-long therapy session. My male therapist was around forty, looked like a runner, and had a gentle manner. We sat at a small round table. There were basic housekeeping issues, privacy documents, and an explanation of the study. And then I talked about myself and why I was there.

My past experience with a therapist when I was in my twenties contrasted greatly with this experience. This time, my therapist did not scribble notes. Instead, he looked directly into my eyes; his total focus was on me. I was being listened to and heard; my grief was acknowledged. *Why, after so many years, was the retelling so painful? Why did it elicit such immense heaves of weeping?*

Putting my thoughts and feelings to words was not easy. The therapist—gentle, patient, well-trained, and knowledgeable—allowed me to proceed gradually, yet he nudged me along through the process. Having never talked about Margie or Jane or grief, I had to learn how.

It was almost too much to process: being in that place, having someone bring up my grief front and center, caring about me so genuinely; the kindness, ease of communication, support, patience, encouragement to take a break if I needed one; my head ping-ponging back and forth, my shoulders hurting from the up-and-down motions of intense crying. By the end of the first session, I had not one morsel of emotional or physical energy left.

Every week I worked on finding activities that reduced stress, provided comfort, and gave me satisfaction or fulfillment. For the first time, the focus was on me. I had to concentrate hard to endure the taxing process of therapy and then shift to restoration mode, which had to include "Judy time." My breaks included ice-skating, walking outside, knitting, playing the piano, reading, visiting the gym, having coffee with a friend, having a dance party with my daughters, and doing crucial work for the success of the annual fundraiser.

Instead of my usual life of always running on autopilot, constantly in motion, the study required me to take a moment to pause and think, *Is this what I want? Am I tired? Do I really need to rush out and exercise now? Can I just chill, read the newspaper, or write in my journal?* I learned how to listen to my body and my emotions, and that type of communication with my inner self helped me to understand a lot about how my emotions set the tone for my day. I was also getting really good at recognizing my triggers. Funerals and cemeteries are triggers for me.

Compassionate Friends has an annual remembrance ceremony in December. Gently encouraged by members of the sibling group, I went, knowing the memorial ceremony could trigger my emotions. Sitting in one of the pews in the back of the Boston church, I tried to listen to the guest speakers. My body involuntarily trembled, which led to sobbing. Unable to handle the intensity, I scooted out and cried all the way home. I realized being there felt like a funeral. I am very selective about which funerals I attend, and I'm always honest with friends if being there is something I cannot handle. What I have learned from my experience is that I need support after attending a funeral. The enormity of my emotions is overwhelming.

I avoided the cemetery like the plague. As part of my intense grief program, my recovery work *required* me to visit the cemetery. *I had to go.*

Terrified at the thought of seeing my sisters' stones again, I was afraid of reliving the crushing emotions I'd felt when I viewed their memorial plaques during my father's funeral. What had happened to me physically then was stuck in the memory of my nervous system—the wrenching sobs and violent trembling and the buckling of my legs, forcing my daughters to nearly carry me back to the car. I didn't know of anyone who would choose to go through that again. Yet, in life, the unexpected challenge often arises and we can only hope we will find the courage to rise to the occasion.

My father passed away in 2011, and his funeral is etched in my brain. He died on a Thursday, and his funeral wasn't until Sunday. I remember the waiting was unbearable. People tried to comfort us with unending, idle chitchat. Chairs in my mother's kitchen scraped like nails on a chalkboard. I'd escaped upstairs.

My friend Lisa called. "What can I bring?"

"Hard candies," I said. "My mouth is so dry from talking. And please, some felt pads for the bottoms of chair legs."

A freaky pre-Halloween snowstorm and power outages

prevented many friends and family from attending my father's funeral. We crunched through the cemetery in snow boots. Adjacent to the hole in the ground awaiting my father's burial, I saw my sisters' memorial plaques for the first time since the day of their funerals thirty and twenty-one years ago. My body convulsed with irrepressible sobs. I could not see or hear a thing. Janie and Amy, on either side of me holding each arm, practically carried me back to the limousine and placed me in the seat. It was too much to bear. Too much loss. Too much sadness. Thirty years of grief exploding.

I had a lot of hesitation about going to the cemetery for my grief study, but I had to do it. The cemetery had a unique layout where the plaques were laid flat to the ground, not upright, and the urns were set into the plaques. The urns could be released to an upright position to resemble a vase for flowers, which I had brought. When Jane's urn got stuck and wouldn't stand up, I felt truly alarmed. But I kept working at it and was finally able to release it to a standing position.

Apropos of a sad day, the weather was cloudy, overcast, and cool. But as I placed the flowers into Jane's urn, the sun unexpectedly burst forth, shining brightly enough to illuminate the words on my sisters' plaques. "She will always live in our hearts," for Jane, and "Rest in peace without pain and with our love," for Margie. The sun continued to shine brightly as I arranged flowers in Margie's urn, and I could not help but think it was a sign. Of what, I was unsure. Perhaps it was a sign of comfort, peace, or simply that my sisters were smiling down on me.

Throughout the grief study program, ice-skating saved me and also connected me to my sisters. One stroke on the ice, one push at a time, my place of meditation. I never felt as free as I did when I was on the ice.

Coincidentally, I had run into a childhood friend, Debbie, on the rink. Our birthdays were only two days apart. We took skating lessons together when we were eight. She still had long, curly blonde hair, just like I remembered. She still owned the replica skating bag from our youth where the two sides of the bag were in the shape of an ice skate. Celebration of Sisters enticed her to skate again. We were back to being two little girls skating in the tiny rink where we started.

I also began teaching beginner's group lessons to children. It was a great way for me to channel my love of ice-skating in a different form. Teaching ice-skating during the five-month period of the grief study allowed me more time on the ice and a break from the grueling therapy. Seeing a child fall numerous times, get up, and finally glide across the ice with a huge smile was such a joy.

"How old are you?" a little boy asked one day as I was helping him lace up his skates. "I think are you are ninety-nine."

"It's not nice to ask a woman her age," I said.

"Well, you're not as old as my grandma. You must be eighty-eight."

A little girl sitting on the bench beside him chirped, "Miss Judy, you have on a different lipstick today."

The children provided such laughter.

In contrast, cognitive behavioral therapy, which required me to relive the days my sisters died, zapped all of my energy. My therapist recorded our sessions as I tried to recall the details of my sisters' deaths, how I heard about their deaths, and what I experienced. These memories had been blocked and buried for years.

"Where were you the day Jane died?" the therapist asked.

At first, I could barely speak.

I tried to get out a few barely audible words between tears and choked breaths. The sound of the clock ticking echoed in my mind. My eyes were perpetually cast down at the table. For fifteen- to twenty-minute blocks of time, I spewed out my guts, but always felt surprised when more details came to the forefront.

Intermittently, the therapist interjected. "What happened next? Is there anything else you remember? You are doing great."

He handed me a CD labeled "Jane" and the date. He assigned me to listen to the recording daily until our next session and indicate how I felt on a chart. We repeated the exercise for weeks, and then repeated the entire process for Margie. *How can I possibly do this?* I thought. But after fifteen minutes, we shifted to restoration and talked about ice-skating, which immediately lifted my spirits.

Per the homework assignment, I placed the CD in the track of my twenty-year-old clock radio console on my nightstand. I sat perched on the edge of my bed. I pressed Play and heard my cracking voice. My tense body struggled to listen, the thumping of my heart the only sound in the room except for my barely audible voice describing the day one of my sisters died. After a few minutes, I had to stop.

Tears filled my blurry eyes again, this time along with hiccups. I needed a break. I needed air. Sunglasses hid my red eyes. I went for a walk on the Charles River to watch the sailing boats. The white caps, the movement, settled me down step by step until my breathing was back to normal, my heartbeat no longer bursting out of my chest.

I started to remember more. I still didn't recall Jane's funeral, but I did remember walking up the hill to Stanetsky's

Funeral Home. Jane's friends got lost and ended up in the Catholic cemetery next to Sharon Memorial Park. Jane would have laughed at that. Talking about Margie's death, I recalled that my cousin John came to visit every day and was incredibly kind.

The therapist and I talked a lot about relinquishing the many aspects of my role as a caretaker. When my sisters died, I became the only daughter left for my parents to lean on. My work in administrative support positions required me to be a caretaker for my bosses throughout my entire working life. As part of my restoration work, therapy taught me to shift the focus from taking care of others to taking care of myself. I needed to figure out what I wanted to do to fulfill my goals and dreams, what kind of work I might aspire to that would not require me to be a caretaker.

I entered the complicated grief study so alone and lost. Clearly, I needed help. The largest hurdle was reflected in my daughter's words when she said grief "defined me." After so many years of silence and secrets and of simply not talking, reversing the cycle would take an immense amount of daily training—not unlike skating. I had to practice, practice, practice. I finally had the guidance to do this immensely challenging work.

CHAPTER 13

Forgiveness

MEMORY: I WAS DRIVING IN THE CAR WHEN I SUDDENLY BROKE DOWN IN TEARS. I WAS NEAR THE NEIGHBORHOOD WHERE WE GREW UP. A MEMORY OF MY SISTERS FLASHED INSTANTLY BEFORE ME. WE WERE RIDING OUR BICYCLES AND LAUGHING. THE SNIPPET WAS GONE IN A SECOND.

My complicated grief program required that I incorporate self-compassion into my practice of forgiveness. I was trained to practice repeating this thought: *I did the best I could at the time. I am amazing now.* These words were crucial.

This was not unlike learning a new element on the ice where I would break down the element into segments, put the pieces back together, and practice the skill over and over hundreds of times until it was mastered. Margie and Jane had been dormant in my life for close to thirty years. My parents wouldn't talk about them, so neither could I. I had shut down, closed doors. My forgiveness training would restore my sisters back into my life and would also restore myself as a functioning human being not "defined by grief." Restoration exercises included looking at photos, telling stories about Margie and Jane, and rereading their precious cards and letters.

Training myself in forgiveness required goals, accountability, and checks and balances. If I cried, I forgave myself for feeling sad. I would look at photos and reflect on them. One photo showed us playing Monopoly on the porch of our first home. *That image is a great way to spark other memories*, I thought, reminding myself that not everything had been lost. If on a particular day I felt exhausted after "spending the day with my sisters," I could take time out to rest. This is what trained athletes do, and it is also what grieving people do. It never stops. Varying degrees of training. Varying degrees of grieving.

Thirty years was half my life. The unrelenting layers of questions, doubts, and what-ifs had spiraled through my head the entire time. When I looked back at the landscape of my life, I recognized that those thirty years could be thought of as "lost time." I tried to rationalize that I did the best I could at that time under the circumstances. And I reminded myself how grateful I was to be undertaking this hard grief work. But my heart would not allow me the freedom of forgiveness. My brain needed an alternative pathway to peace.

I reread the rabbi's eulogy from Jane's funeral. He had said, "There is no satisfactory answer to understanding why bad things happen to good people. Not all questions have answers. Unanswered "whys" are a part of life. The way to face tragedy is with love. Use the love we had for Jane to forgive ourselves." Focusing on his words helped me knock down roadblocks to forgiving myself.

Regrets was another word associated with forgiveness. I had so many regrets I could have built a house of them. Why didn't I reach out to someone? Why didn't I embrace the siblings from Compassionate Friends? Why didn't I talk about my sisters? What if I had not moved back to be closer to my parents? Why did it take thirty years to finally start the grieving process? The laundry list went on and on, but it was not productive. The hamster wheel would never stop.

To forgive was to be resilient. I needed to channel forgiveness to my brain and heart. I needed to show compassion for myself—not only my current self but also my younger self, who, despite the odds, did more than okay. Where I had once exhibited patterns of shutting down and closing doors—a result of my parents' inability to talk about my sisters passed down to me—now I was trying to embrace forgiveness. Slowly, doors were opening to new opportunities, and I was learning to welcome them.

In 2017, I was about to perform in Ice Chips, an annual figure skating show hosted by the Skating Club of Boston held at the ice arena at Harvard University. I performed in two numbers: the Bostonians, a decades-long tradition of Ice Chips where a group of a dozen adults performs a synchronized number, and the Adult number choreographed for members over the age of eighteen. I never experienced the excitement of a full-blown show with talented skaters in glamorous costumes that was reminiscent of the ice shows I attended with my sisters when we were young.

There was so much energy in the air. The Margie in me applied the black eyeliner. The dress rehearsal was exciting as all of us got ready in our assigned dressing room, waited backstage, and heard our number announced throughout the arena. I recall the first practice when the lights went out, and there was darkness at the conclusion of our performance. I stopped in my tracks because I wasn't able to skate in the dark. I had an instant flashback of Jane's death and awakening to total darkness. I froze, feeling petrified. One of my fellow skaters took my hand and guided me off the ice. Thankfully, that happened during practice.

The live performances were great! When I first saw my costume of silver and gold glitz, which barely covered my rear end, I gasped. Never in my life had I worn a skirt so short, though we did wear bike shorts underneath. I slipped on the dress with all its sparkle.

Judy, you look beautiful! I heard my sisters calling.

Funny how I still cannot erase the memory of my experience as a young girl when I had to have my clothing altered. Whenever Margie and I needed alterations to our clothes, we visited a dressmaker who always wore a housecoat, blue slippers, and her gray hair in tight pin curls. The floor, always cold, was black-and-white-checkered linoleum. We climbed three steps to a landing, then stepped up one more level to the full-length mirror. Tapping her yardstick on the floor, the dressmaker commanded us to turn as she pinned up our dresses or made white chalk marks on the material. She deemed what dress lengths were appropriate. Margie's dresses just covered her rear end while mine were hemmed just above my knees. "Your legs are too fat," the dressmaker said, a comment that crushed my spirit and stayed with me always.

It was the irony of life. For as long as I could remember, I only wanted to be like Margie—to look like her, to ice-skate like her, and to wear short skirts like her. Thirty years later, I was doing all of that and I couldn't have cared less. I would have given it all back in a heartbeat. All I wanted was my Margie back. When Margie died, I lost my soulmate, a sister who truly knew me and my inner thoughts, and who set me on the right course. We had shared our lives, and I still missed the laughter, disagreements, and conversations that would last for hours.

Jane and I never had the opportunity to discover each other fully or deepen our relationship. In my fantasies, I imagined watching our children grow up together, sharing milestones, celebrating holidays, the two of us having sisterly arguments, shouldering the burden of aging parents, and talking on the telephone for hours on end.

But healing has taken place—through forgiveness and in acknowledging regret. After my sisters died, I never spoke of it. Now when I meet someone new, I say, "I am the middle of three. Sadly, I lost both of my sisters."

CHAPTER 14

Traditions: Old, New, and Revised

MEMORY: ONE YEAR, IN MY TWENTIES, I CAME HOME FROM NEW YORK CITY TO CELEBRATE MY BIRTHDAY—WITHOUT A BIRTHDAY CAKE. THE FOLLOWING YEAR, MY MOTHER CALLED A FRIEND TO REMIND HER TO GET ME A CAKE. WHAT IS A BIRTHDAY WITHOUT A CAKE?

Every Mother's Day, I would wake up with a knot in the pit of my stomach. My full focus was always on my mother and how horrific the day must be for her. For a short time, she and I exchanged cards. But standing in a store reading Hallmark cards would stir up too many emotions. The humorous cards seemed ridiculous and the deep-meaning ones too sad. After several years, we abandoned this. My daughters always presented me with beautiful and thoughtful cards and did their best to make the day special. But I was always distracted, worrying about my own mother.

Then one of my daughters came up with an idea. How about celebrating Mother's Day on another day? Brilliant! My head could be clear, I could savor being the proud mother of Janie and Amy, and my daughters and I could focus on being together.

Birthdays were also difficult. My family held parties to mark my milestone fortieth and fiftieth birthdays, though I could never fully enjoy the experience. But I knew how much the parties meant to my daughters, so I forced myself to put on a good face while my heart was broken because my sisters were not there. That was one of the reasons why my fifty-fifth birthday gift to the Dorothy Hamill skating camp was so special. It was such a beautiful, transformative experience, and I was able to let go and just be me.

There was always a cloud hanging over my birthdays. The last time I saw Jane was over Columbus Day weekend in 1981, and we celebrated my twenty-fifth birthday. My memory of that weekend is hazy. I came home for a wedding our entire family attended. I don't recall many details. I do remember Jane and I went shopping. We had the typical bickering over who was going to drive down Commonwealth Avenue in Boston, and for once I won. I can still see Jane's face sitting next to me in the front seat of the car, smiling with that dimple on her cheek. I now associate my birthday with the loss of my dear sister Jane, the final time I saw her, and the last time the Lipson family of five would be together.

We had amazing birthday parties when we were kids. I have many memories of us as kids housed in the basement of our home on Indian Ridge Road. I loved our birthday parties, dressing up in party dresses, those silly party hats with elastic to secure on your head, streamers, cake and ice cream, presents, and happy times.

Margie was always unique. For her ninth birthday, the invitations read, "Come dressed as your father." She pulled her hair back into a ponytail and wore my father's suit jacket and tie. The jacket hung over Margie's shoulders and dangled down to her ankles. My father took a black-and-white Polaroid of every dressed-up child, which was given to them as a party favor. In Margie's picture she looks perplexed about wearing this costume. Pictures from other birthday parties show Margie and the other children having a good time, wearing party hats, and sitting around a long rectangular table eating Hoodsie Cups of chocolate and vanilla ice cream. On cue for the camera, Margie would jazz it up with her vivacious smile.

Like Margie, I celebrated my birthdays in our basement. I loved that our party dresses often matched each other, making us sisters feel united and close. The same rectangular table was set up with paper party goods. We ate chicken from Fontaine's—a favorite before Kentucky Fried Chicken—birthday cake and Hoodsies, and then played pin the tail on the donkey.

We also had happy times at Anthony's Pier 4, a landmark restaurant on the South Boston Waterfront. It was famous for its hot, crisp, golden popovers. A pirate with a wooden leg would open the heavy wooden door as we entered, hoping to secure a table next to the window to watch the boats sailing in and out of the harbor.

Before the birthday cake arrived, my mother always asked, "Does anyone need the ladies' room?"

"Yes!" we chorused, leaving my poor father at the table alone. Single file, we marched through the restaurant, over the little bridge where the lobsters swam, to the ladies' room, perpetually arguing over who would go first. Then the dash back to our father. My father dealt with all of our moods and recognized the special, unique qualities in each of us—Margie's intelligence, wit, gumption, and tenacity; my quiet resilience yet determination to make my mark; and Jane's spunk combined with naïveté and assertiveness. I was very grateful to have those memories.

Starting in 2013, I started reframing my birthday so it didn't carry so much heavy emotional weight. For my fifty-seventh birthday, my daughters, my best friend, and I traveled to New

York City. I was ready to start a new tradition. "Jane would want you to be happy and celebrate on your birthday," a friend of Jane's said, and I repeated that mantra over and over every year in the weeks leading up to my birthday.

From Boston, we took the train and stayed right in the heart of the New York City where I'd flourished in my twenties. I loved showing my daughters my old haunts and taking them into Bloomingdale's where I had worked. Veering down a new avenue or seeing a Broadway show did shift the focus and ease some of the deep pain. It felt good to blend old traditions with new ones.

"Mommy, you doing okay?" my daughters asked. They looked directly into my eyes.

"I'm doing great," I said, and I was.

We went to the Century 21 Department Store where I told the girls they could each select a handbag as my gift. The sea of bags flowed through three large rooms. They chose numerous handbags that I hung on my arms until I couldn't carry any more. Finally, each girl selected their prize bag. We all shared a room, picked up some candy—much like I had done with my sisters—and shared some laughs while people watching. From time to time, I felt a pang of sadness, but I also rejoiced in the joy of being with my daughters.

On what would have been Jane's sixtieth birthday, I received a lovely email from her friend Pam. "If Jane were alive," Pam wrote, "we would still be wonderful friends laughing at the thought of turning sixty." Pam said she thought about Jane a lot and missed the special times they shared. I can still see them as little girls in elementary school with the cute pixie haircuts swinging on the swings in our backyard.

There's a beautiful photo of Jane dressed up as a flapper from the 1920s with bright red lipstick, white-flowered headband,

and a white flapper dress, flashing her beaming smile. Jane and her friends were celebrating, lots of loud laughter, with Jane at the center, the life of the party, touching each and every person there.

Milestone birthdays were particularly hard, so I marked them with something I loved. For my sixtieth, I signed up for an adult skating camp in Sun Valley, Idaho. I wanted to celebrate with a real, old-fashioned ice-skating party. Not all of my friends skated, so we had a party room with refreshments and fun overlooking the rink. The day of the party, I crashed. I told a dear friend I didn't think I could go through with it. She talked me off the ledge. I was glad she did.

The outdoor rink had some of the best views overlooking breathtaking mountains. Ice dancing in the twilight among glistening stars in a dark sky was a new, unforgettable experience. Skating with a world champion at camp, I could not help but think once again, *Am I dreaming?*

My ice-skating pals and I took to the ice. We turned up the music and formed a kick line, dancing on the ice. Smiles beaming, including my own. We had the time of our lives. Some watched from above in awe. A few took to the ice after years of not being on skates.

"This is the first skating party I have ever been to," said one friend. "This is a blast!"

I took a moment to look around—friends from all facets of my life were present. For the first time, I had planned this party because it was the way *I* wanted to celebrate my birthday.

There was more to celebrate in 2018. My older daughter, Janie, was engaged, and my younger daughter, Amy, was getting married that year. It was a wonderful opportunity to invite cousins to the bridal shower and wedding. All were delighted to celebrate such a happy occasion with us. As soon as we said hello and hugged, it felt like time had vanished. We reminisced about our childhoods—large Chanukah parties, sleepovers, and tales of our grandparents. We shared our versions of my great-aunt, who frequently asked if I had a boyfriend. I felt so grateful to restore these relationships and have my cousins back in my life.

Just like so many other milestone years—whether happy or sad—my emotions imploded. I missed Margie and Jane even more deeply and yearned to have them with me. But this time was different. I felt happy, even excited, to live my life in the present moment while acknowledging the past.

CHAPTER 15

We Get Up

MEMORY: I DONNED A PINK DRESS LACED WITH YELLOW AND GLITTER STUD EARRINGS TO TAKE MY BRONZE MOVES IN THE FIELD FIGURING SKATING TEST. GAZING INTO THE MIRROR, I RECOGNIZED MY RESEMBLANCE TO MARGIE AND JANE.

It was March 2018, and I was about to practice a spin on the ice. My skates newly sharpened, I skated to the end of the rink near the mirrors in a spot away from the fast skaters. One foot crossed over the other, I stepped into the spin, one arm overhead, the other arm extended, and then—*nothing.*

Complete darkness.

I had fallen. I had hit the side of my head, suffered a concussion, bruised the entire left side of my face, and cut the corner of my eye, requiring eight stitches. I learned later that two coaches had lifted me up, each holding me under one arm, and glided me off the ice, sitting me down on a bench. I had no clue how my ice skates were removed, how my handbag was retrieved, and no recollection of the ambulance ride to the hospital.

Little did I know this accident would take me off the ice for three months and that I would not regain my stamina or completely recover for a full year.

Weekly visits to the doctor to assess my progress and a daily log describing my symptoms made me realize the severity of my injuries. The ice was not forgiving, said my doctor, and he did not want me—at the age of sixty-one—to return to the sport I loved.

The prospect of not being able to skate horrified and saddened me. I could not fathom my life without ice-skating. The ice was my connection to my beloved sisters. Would that mean I'd have to cancel my performance in Celebration of Sisters? Skating was my passion and a means of meditation. Without it, I would be lost.

I had to be patient, which was not one of my virtues. The Get Up campaign, which was launched by the U.S. Figure Skating Association in 2017, recognizes the "grit, passion, and perseverance" that every skater needs to get up and go to the rink every day. I did everything I could to live by that code, but it was hard with an injury. But I had no choice but to try as hard as I could to persevere. I was very inspired by Learn to Skate USA's manifesto:

Ice skaters learn more than ice skating.
They learn sharper focus, wilder creativity,
   and what it feels like to really fly.
Ice-skating teaches children and their parents
That with a little imagination,
A dash of confidence,
And a brush of bravery
They can soar
Towards making their dreams come true.
That they can make their
Mark on the world
And that they can skate to great—one blade at a time.

I eventually returned to the ice with fierce determination and proved the naysayers wrong. At first, physically and mentally, I couldn't even do my usual daily activities like working out, reading, watching TV, using my electronic devices, and driving my car. One of the few things I could do every day was walk.

My first day back at the rink, I had no expectations. I laced up my skates, put one tentative foot on the ice, then the other, and off I went on a slow lap around the rink. How I had missed the cool breeze in my hair, the smell of the rink, and being with other skaters. All I managed was basic stroking, but that was more than I had anticipated. Piece by piece, step by step, one hurdle at a time, *I would do this.*

The crushing fall and recovery kept me off the ice for three months—an extremely long time for any skater, especially an adult skater. As I prepared for the eighth annual Celebration of Sisters in 2018, I returned with purpose, and some frustration. I took a very minor tumble, which is natural for the sport, but it rattled me. I was unable to get my groove back. My head was full of old thoughts; I lacked nerve and felt unsteady.

One month before the event, my coach Linda and I discussed my skating.

"Why do you skate?" she asked.

"I skate because I love it!" I said. "I skate for myself, my sisters, and for the joy."

Whenever I put that hat on, it shows in my skating—and that day in training, it certainly did. I felt empowered, strong, and happy on the ice again. No one cared how I skated, nor did I care—nor should I care. The important thing was why I skated and what skating meant to me.

I stepped onto the ice with gusto.

Two weeks before Celebration of Sisters, I had a total meltdown. While performing a dress rehearsal in my new purple dress, all the emotions I had suppressed after my terrible fall came crashing in. My mind was overwhelmed by thoughts—the realization of the seriousness of my head injury and the fact that, despite the injury, *I was here* and skating in memory of my sisters. I felt super nervous, extremely tentative, insecure. Definitely not as strong.

I skated a shaky run-through. Ironically, I completed the final spin that traditionally posed a problem. But my legs shook. Tears kept me from finishing the session. I needed to get out of the skating dress. I could not breathe.

For the first time, the ice had not ignited its magic solace.

My coach Linda was extremely patient. Usually, our preparation for Celebration of Sisters started in June. She'd typically listen to the music and choreograph a piece that showcased both the theme of the lyrics and my skating ability. Week after week, we'd practice. In front of the mirror at the end of the rink, I went through my arm movements, ensuring they looked graceful. She once asked if I took ballet as a young girl. "With this body and coordination," I said, "do I look like I took ballet?" Concentrating on the music and steps, I tended to rush and my arms would look robotic.

In the end, I skated a magnificent number with lots of edges in the Celebration of Sisters 2018 event. I was so grateful to be able to skate and to pay tribute to Margie and Jane. In reality, Celebration of Sisters would have happened whether or not I performed, but my skating was the glue to the event for me. My skating was the piece of my grief journey that led me back to Margie and Jane, and after so many years, I was delighted to share my sisters with everyone.

My significant piece was a spiral where I lifted one leg up high and skated across the ice, arms stretched out, head held high. I felt Margie and Jane on either side, gliding with me on the cool ice.

My family and ice-skating—not grief—defined my life. The rink was my happy place, my safe place, my sanctuary. Since my accident, I was a bit more cautious, consciously staying in my zone. But serenity and excitement still took hold the moment I grabbed my skates, slid my feet into them, laced them up, and hit the rink. Whether alone or with fellow skaters, tranquility flowed through my body as the Zamboni circled the ice, smoothing as it went.

This type of tenacity of never giving up reminded me of my childhood with my sisters. We used to love swimming, but no matter how cold we were, we always dove back in. We belonged to a pool club twenty minutes from our house. Several family friends with kids our age also belonged to the club. To swim in the deep end with the cool slide, you had to pass a swim test, several laps required. We had many fun times there with the exception of others making fun of my "chubbiness." My sisters and I splashed in the pool with our friends, stunning in our gorgeous white bathing caps.

Margie and I were adept at swimming and had a thrill of carrying Jane around in the pool. We made a chair with our hands—just like the day of the nor'easter—and pranced around the pool with Jane sitting like our little doll. We stayed in the water until our lips turned blue, forcing us to warm up in the sun, wrapped in towels, anxiously awaiting jumping back in.

Lessons learned on the ice often transferred to life. My coach once asked me to trace the same line over and over. Making figure eights and tracking your exact line is not as easy as it sounds. In my complicated grief work, I had to go over the deaths of my sisters for many weeks, reliving the days they died. Tracing the lines over and over, just like figure eights, helped me remember more and more.

Another lesson was the importance of getting up after a fall, which I learned numerous times. No matter what, in life and in skating, when you fall you must get up. Perhaps I needed this at the forefront of my mind to forgive myself for delaying thirty years before I did my grief work.

The community of skaters I found and the environment of the ice-skating arena have afforded me a constant connection to Margie and Jane, have provided me with both a literal and metaphorical "circle of comfort," and have helped me secure my identity as the middle sister and a person I never thought I could be: someone with enough backbone to get out there and perform.

CHAPTER 16

It Is Never Too Late to Grieve

MEMORY: I STEPPED ON THE ICE, THE QUIET, THE CLEAR, SHEER GLEAMING SURFACE; LEGS SHAKING, TENTATIVE, ONE FOOT AT A TIME. I COULD DO THIS. I COULD SKATE, AND I COULD GRIEVE FOR MARGIE AND JANE.

On a warm July day in 2019, I held onto the boards that surround the rink for balance and with trepidation stepped onto the ice. My feet and legs were a bit wobbly, but with a push of the narrow blade, I was off, flying with the breeze in my hair. It took a few laps to warm up, for my knees to soften, for my shoulders to relax, and to secure my footing. Every step a reminder of skating with my sisters, I envisioned Margie wearing her short skating dress, Jane in her short, blonde bob— my circle of comfort, my circling around the rink, circling to my sisters.

There had been a hiatus of ten days since I'd been on the ice, which was a substantial lack of practice for a sixty-two-year-old. I was definitely off my game. As I warmed up, my body shook and I was crying. Puzzled by the reaction, I stroked around until I got my legs back.

When I got home from skating, I settled down on the couch and thought about what had happened. Why did I have such an overwhelming emotional reaction on the ice?

Eight days prior, I was in New York celebrating the birth of my first grandchild, named after my beloved father, Benjamin. Holding the sleeping baby boy for the first time after a long procession of girls, I'd whispered, "Hi, Benji, it's your Nini." He opened his eyes and looked directly at me. I melted, an instant and forever love.

The first day I went back to work after Margie and Jane died, I'd experienced the same reaction that I'd had on the ice— shaking and crying. Back then, I'd felt devastating grief. But now, after Benji's birth, I felt absolute, full-blown joy. Two ends of a spectrum.

The death of my sisters changed me. The birth of my Benji changed me.

It is never too late to grieve. Grief comes in waves.

When I sold my suburban home in 2011 after twenty years, coinciding with my work on grief, I was forced to downsize and sift through boxes that sat untouched for nineteen years in my basement. I was elated to discover a box of photographs and letters from my sisters. It felt like opening a precious gift; I relished each piece as I carefully unwrapped one photo at a time, one letter at a time. The process in 2011 looked very different from the process in 2019.

When Jane died, I frantically assembled a collage of photos. My thinking was somewhat delusional; somehow, I felt the pictures would bring my sister back. In that moment, I panicked that everything relating to Margie and Jane would be lost. I was rummaging through my parents' home the week of the Shiva. I had to take the photos back with me to New York. After Margie died, I was even more frantic as I repeated the process. The collage was a montage of Margie, me, and Jane throughout the years with various configurations: Margie with me, Margie with

Jane, me with Jane, and all three sisters together. I feverishly cut the pictures to fit the squares into each box of the frame.

When I went through the complicated grief program, I was forced to open boxes of memories, literally and figuratively. But something happened to me on the ice in July 2019—a major shift in my grief. My sadness had transformed.

I broke out the box of photos again, ready to relive precious memories of my sisters. The more I poured over the scattered photos, letters, and cards—repeatedly and with great gusto—the more I clung to Margie and Jane, the prism reflecting so colorfully what it meant to be a sister. The connection remained, despite the horrible fights, darkest challenges, joyous celebrations, and the deepest love, out of which arose the knowledge that a sister would walk through fire and be there for you no matter what. Nothing and no one could replace that relationship. This is what I will always cling to.

I was not afraid to look at the pictures. Every view was unique, every emotion varied, every experience volatile. *What were we thinking? What was the mood? Who took the picture?* Sometimes I remembered. Sometimes I did not. The regrets of not grieving sooner and the haunting inability to remember many details had dissipated, and I was discovering more about my sisters and myself.

I allowed myself to feel whatever was flowing. I never realized the strong resemblance I had to both Margie and Jane, which makes me sad and makes my heart expand with pride at the same time. I need to be kinder to myself for not remembering and cherish what I do recall, two beautiful sisters.

Jane was the extrovert and life of the party, but the pictures depicted a serious side. Margie endured many years of grueling pain, yet there was always a gorgeous smile in the photos. I was the epitome of the middle child, an independent thinker and always on the perimeter. Remembering my sisters as they were, rather than putting them on imaginary pedestals, helped me grieve them as individuals.

In one photo of Jane, age three, she was wearing Danskin pants and fluffy slippers, posed in a little girl stance, expanding her little belly against the wall in our basement. The picture was similar to a photo of my daughters posing in my parents' home. Jane was fairer than Margie and me, just absolutely precious. She held her favorite Susie Q doll, a tiny doll with blonde hair and many outfits. Jane's little-girl sweetness contrasted in my mind with her human quality of being mean-spirited at times.

In another photo, all three of us—ages nine, seven, and four—wore party dresses, white lace ankle socks, black patent leather Mary Janes, and puffy winter coats. In Boston Common, Margie gregariously ran after the birds with her peanuts. I stood back, a bit contemplative, not quite sure what to do. Jane was carefree, skipping around, throwing her peanuts to the birds. This captured the personalities of all the Lipson sisters.

Did it matter what Jane's and Margie's favorite colors or foods were? What games we played on the porch? Compiling these kinds of details would not bring my sisters back. I had to relinquish my need to elicit every tiny detail. I needed to look at the big picture, yet I couldn't break away from the photographs.

One of my favorites was of Margie taken by a professional photographer and touched up with makeup. Margie, a twinkle in her eye, held a large red telephone, showing her love for the gift of the gab at an early age. Margie was the consummate talker, making nonstop conversation with everyone she encountered. Often, this drove me crazy.

Another favorite was taken at my wedding. With huge broad smiles, tightly holding onto each other, Margie and I hugged, looking directly into each other's eyes. The wedding was over and I had changed out of my gown into a going-away outfit. Margie knew I was so thankful for her presence. I had no other attendants, only my big sister. It meant the world to both of us. Margie wanted me to go into the next chapter of my life happy, despite her pain. In many situations, Margie and I did not need to speak. No words. *We knew.*

In high school, Jane attended a formal in a long, navy gown. She stood in our living room, one hand on the baby grand piano. Now, a double take. *Was this a picture of Jane or me?* The girl at the piano could easily have been me in college.

The photo of me with my father when he came up for my college's "Happy Pappy" weekend could be a ringer for my sister Jane. I wore a long, navy-blue dress and a white corsage on my wrist. I looked forward to this time with my father. Socials, dinners, and tours of the campus filled the weekend. My father and I had similar natures—we did not prefer the social activities, so we did a little shopping, hung out together, and we never lacked for conversation. With my closest friend and her father, we dressed up and tried to attend the formal dance, but it was not our cup of tea. The four of us, all decked out, ditched the dance and went to Friendly's for ice cream cones.

There was a picture of our three beaming smiles at an April 1981 casino party in honor of our father's fiftieth birthday. Jane, flanked by Margie and me, wore a purple sleeveless dress, her light brown hair in bangs, the dimple on her cheek prominent in her smile. Margie looked physically well. I wore a long-sleeve, two-piece red silk outfit. All three Lipson sisters looked stunning. This is one of my favorite pictures. Jane was my sweet, adorable younger sister, Margie looked gorgeous in her precise black eyeliner, and the three of us were together.

Today, with all that I have lost, I am so grateful for all that I have gained. I am incredibly sad that my Margie and Jane are not here to share my beautiful new grandson—and any more grandchildren I might have—with me. But my heart is full with new family, extended family, a new precious life, a new beginning, and a new love.

The truth, revealed after several years of grief work, was that everything was so complex. Grief involved change, which was not easy for individuals in a situation where roles in the family, expectations, and patterns of behavior had already been established. There were differences between my need for solitude and my being set aside by my family to manage my grief by myself. I had gone through life feeling alone, lost, lonely, and barely surviving in my grief. Change was not easy, but with the support of those involved in the complicated grief study, my daughters, my friends—and ice-skating—it was possible. The clear, smooth ice was my blank canvas.

Margie and Jane are now and forever at the forefront of my mind—the circles of comfort are complete. My sisters are gone, but they remain in my life, my legacy, my being. The lost memories haunted me for thirty years. Today, sweet memories come alive. We were fondly known as the three Lipson sisters, and we still are. Always three.

EPILOGUE

Celebration of Sisters

MEMORY: THERE IS NO ONE LIKE A SISTER. MY SISTERS ARE MY CONSTANT CHEERLEADERS, CHAMPIONS, AND COMPETITORS. I AM A SISTER. *WE ARE FOREVER: MARGIE, JUDY, JANE.*

The Celebration of Sisters ice-skating fundraiser provides the greatest rediscovery and reconnection to my sisters. At the time of this writing, there have been nine events, with the grand finale scheduled in 2021. Year after year, the legacies of Margie and Jane are shared with a growing community.

The preparation for Celebration of Sisters commences the day after the event of the previous year and amps up five to six months prior to the following event. It's a true labor of love, yet filled with many mixed emotions. A very tiny piece in my head spins the fact that I even have to do an event to commemorate the lives and memories of sisters. I try not to focus on that.

What began in November 2012 as ten figure skaters in a rink with one set of bleachers has grown to seventy-five figure skaters with an audience of almost two hundred people. At the time of this writing, we have raised more than $60,000 to benefit Massachusetts General Hospital.

I decided from the start that the show would not showcase famous skaters, but instead would spotlight figure skaters of all ages, levels, and disciplines. The music is carefully chosen. Performances have included single skaters, pairs, ice dancers, synchronized skating teams, and skaters from the Special

Olympics. I tried to design the Celebration of Sisters event to reflect what it truly means to be a sister.

Choosing a song that I would perform to at the Celebration of Sisters event was always a thoughtful process. All year long, I'd listen to dozens of songs in search of the perfect one. Much of my grief comes in waves, my mind floating in and out of water, like the force of the tides. The same feeling paralleled every year of the Celebration of Sisters event, a different wave based on the year, the date, and the selection of music. First, the song had to reflect the gala's themes: sisters, love, loss, and celebration. Second, it had to convey the perfect rhythm to ice-skate to. Above all, I needed to love the lyrics.

In 2014, I skated my first solo when I was fifty-eight. In a red skating dress, hair coiffed, makeup done, nails painted red, I posed in the center of the arena. With over a hundred people focused on me, my nerves escalated to an all-new level of shakiness. Thirty seconds into "What a Feeling" from *Flashdance*, I froze. I forgot the choreography. *What should I do?* In my mind, an eternity passed; in reality, probably only five seconds. Somehow, I had the stamina to keep moving, muddling through the steps. I was supposed to look at the audience, but instead looked down at my feet as if they might tell me what to do. At the end, my face expressed mixed relief and disappointment. I attempted to smile and took a bow.

I can only envision my two sisters giggling, but hopefully they were proud that Judy, the shy middle sister, had performed in front of a large audience. Celebration of Sisters "makes it happen," I thought, just like the lyrics say. Images of us sisters—Margie, me, and Jane—ice-skating, enjoying the music, and sharing love danced in my brain and "took hold of my heart."

The date of the Celebration of Sisters event in 2015 fell on Margie's birthday, and for the first time, I chose to skate in two numbers. The dress selection for that sentimental year had to be pink, Margie's favorite color, with a splash of yellow, Jane's favorite color.

Can this be me? I thought as I stood in front of a mirror wearing a tight-fitting, sparkly dress cut several inches above my knee. *Is this the girl who stood in the wings?* Judy, the middle sister, forever overshadowed by Margie and Jane. Judy, the shy, chubby sister who cried in the dressing room in Jordan Marsh attempting to purchase a dress for her bat mitzvah. Judy, who sat in her room, reading alone when Margie went to parties and Jane gabbed on the phone with friends. As I stared at myself in the mirror, I really looked at myself—my eyes, my nose, my mouth, the expression on my face. Tears poured down my cheeks as I saw a strong resemblance to Margie and a confidence in myself I had never seen before.

The song I chose that year was "We Will Never Be Apart," written by J. Michael Call and Colette Call Lofgren. Week after week, as I practiced, I cried often, as did my coach. I had never ice-skated to such a dauntingly emotional piece of music and lyrics.

I stepped onto the ice, dedicating the performance to my sisters and all lost siblings. As "We Will Never Be Apart" played, I skated robotically, my body so tense it could not flow with the music, my shoulders hunched up to my ears. Hearing the lyrics to the song on Margie's birthday was almost more than I could handle, and my body could not ease into the flow of the blade. The second I stepped off the ice, I wept.

We Will Never Be Apart

How do I go on without you?
How will I ever smile again?
How can I live when all that I love is torn from my side?
How can I find hope without you?
You, who have been my truest friend
Lifting my soul through heartache and fear
Again and again
We will never be apart, we're sisters
I will always be there by your side
There are simply bonds that can't be broken
By distance or time
There won't be a day when I'm not with you
You will always be safe in my heart
Waiting for that world when at last
Our sorrows are past
But until that time
We will never be apart.

The next skate was to one of Margie's favorite songs, "Downtown," sung by Petula Clark. We skated a fun, sassy number, hamming it up just like my Margie always had. My pink dress was complemented by yellow dresses worn by the four girls who skated with me. We donned paisley headbands that flowed down our backs, reflecting the time period of the sixties. I imagined my Margie playing her guitar as we danced on the ice to her lovely voice singing the song.

At the end of the show, Margie's dearest friend Michael approached me, eyes brimming with tears. He said he'd done a double take when I was skating because I looked so much like Margie. This felt like the greatest compliment I'd ever received.

We hugged. The comfort of his presence and acknowledgement of Margie's life and memory gave me a renewed commitment to continue the Celebration of Sisters event. From that point on, however, I avoided skating to such harrowingly emotional pieces of music. Instead, I picked tunes that were more upbeat.

The song I chose for my performance in 2016's Celebration of Sisters felt so right as I continued to rediscover and redefine myself through grief work. Billy Porter's rendition of "I've Gotta Be Me" was drilled into my brain and life as I practiced, and once I had the performance down, I truly felt the freedom to be me.

The 2016 event was our sixth; it fell on Jane's birthday. I skated to Carole King's "Beautiful." Both Margie and Jane were Carole King fans and beautiful inside and out. In honor of Jane, the number performed in a trio and repeated as a solo a few years later.

I wore a new dress of light blue fabric with a lace overlay studded with many sparkling stones, which weighed down the dress enough that I had to practice a few times before the show to make sure I felt comfortable. I'd never had a dress of this caliber before. I also realized that perhaps I was beginning to perceive my loss differently than before. Perhaps the depth of my loss was easing a bit. I recognized now, in my heart, that my sisters had never been truly lost to me. Margie's and Jane's voices were instilled in my own.

They were me. And I was them.

On the day of the event, I was on autopilot. I arrived at the rink three hours early and skated for a brief warm-up, all dolled up in my pretty dress and makeup, my body free of nerves. Then the friendly deliveryman arrived with the water and large bouquet of balloons, so I flew off the ice to put them away. I raced around—to place signs around the rink, meet and greet volunteers and skaters, and take care of everything else. My adrenaline was off the charts.

By four thirty, the guests had filled the bleachers. On the ice, surrounded by our largest group of skaters yet, seventy-five, I addressed the audience. First, I thanked them for their generosity, and then I told them about my sisters, Margie and Jane.

What anxiety! My mouth was parched, my voice cracked, and I could barely breathe. I had trouble juggling the microphone and the speech in my hands because I was shaking and crying. Finally, I handed the microphone back to the master of ceremonies. In one minute, I had to join the others to skate the opening number.

"You have this," said the emcee.

"All is good to go," said the skating manager.

Seventy-five skaters open with "Over the Rainbow," the lovely rendition by Israel Kamakawiwo'ole, a gorgeous sea of color flowing around the rink. The applause as I joined the skaters echoed love, warmth, and support for me and my sisters. It was utterly overwhelming.

People later told me I delivered my strongest performance ever, which I attributed to muscle memory, practice, and the presence of my sisters. Halfway through "Beautiful" by Carole King, I felt my body settle down and enjoyed my skating. Though I fumbled on a few elements, the audience was none the wiser. The sparkling finale was danced to "Up—Up & Away," sung by the 5th Dimension.

"Please welcome back the entire cast of Celebration of Sisters!" the master of ceremonies announced.

The skaters headed onto the ice with balloons tied to their hands, an array of color floating above. *Am I dreaming?* I thought, not for the first time, and imagined my sisters and me skating together and laughing.

"Would you like to ride in my beautiful balloon?" The skaters performed one final element. Then, one by one, gathered in the center of the rink, balloons fluttering high.

Then I got my cue, a beautiful song lyric about chasing my dreams across the sky. I skated onto the ice with a dozen balloons. I did a spiral—standing on one leg, lifting the other high off the ice. I held Margie's and Jane's hands as they made my dream come true.

Altogether, we raised our arms up and took our final bow. The balloons soared up then down in a sea of gorgeous color. What a spectacular closing tribute to Margie and Jane. My emotions collided. I felt the push and pull of celebrating my sisters and simultaneously missing them. I did not hear the applause. I was so deeply focused on the music, skating, and my sisters. I was focused on how I felt in that moment, of how far I'd come.

I feel profoundly proud after each Celebration of Sisters event, recognizing that the event itself has helped me find permission to feel all of these emotions—and to sense that Margie and Jane are with me, guiding me.

I have learned many life lessons from ice-skating. The lines on the ice scratched and etched by narrow silver blades either in a straight line or circles. The trajectory and designs on the shining surface are sometimes perfectly symmetrical and oftentimes not how I wanted life to be.

Grief is part of me, but I hope that grief no longer defines me. Sadly, I did lose my sisters Margie and Jane. I will always miss them and have a permanent hole in my heart. My sisters are part of me: my past, my present, and my future.

This is the story of a shy middle girl who emerged from the back seat to take center stage of her life with the help of many, and how ice-skating helped guide her along the way.

I am the ice-skater—the sister, the mother, the daughter, the woman—who fell and got up.

Author's Note

From its inception in November 2011, the Celebration of Sisters ice-skating gala has brought me full circle to a place where I have been able to honor and remember my sisters, positively channel my grief, heal, and find a community of loving people for whom I will always be grateful.

If, by hearing my story, another person who has lost a sibling does not feel so alone, we've done good. If, by attending or hearing about the gala, a new skater stands up, we've done good. If an individual learns about advocating for healthcare, we've done good. If someone with an eating disorder or that person's family member or friend seeks help, we've done good. If we have brought joy, we've done good.

Thank you to the donors, skaters, coaches, volunteers, and vendors who generously supported this event for the past decade. I am forever grateful.

Acknowledgments

Thank you to all who have supported this project. My deepest gratitude goes to Elizabeth Mearkle-Cumming for providing me with the impetus to write after my father, Benjamin Lipson, died in 2011.

To Dr. John Goodson for encouraging me to tell Margie and Jane's story when we first established the Marjorie E. and Jane E. Memorial Fund at Massachusetts General Hospital in 1999. You said people needed to know about my sisters, and now they will.

As a debut memoir, thank you to my extraordinary team of coaches and editors for your encouragement, wisdom, knowledge, guidance, and direction: Caroline Leavitt, Robyn Ringler, and Marion Roach Smith. To the team at the Open to Hope Foundation for the wonderful work you do and supporting my work: Neil Chethik, Harriet Hodgson, Dr. Heidi Horsley, Gloria Horsley, and Heather Horsley.

Thank you to WriteLife Publishing and the team who assisted a debut author. You were all incredibly generous, kind, and helped me navigate the process with such ease: Terri Leidich, Julie Bromley, John Daly, Allison Itterly, Andrea Vande Vorde, Rebecca Lown, Robin Krauss, and Glenn Leidich.

To my close circle of friends, you know who you are, my true treasures for being there for me all these years. Now you will learn my complete story. To my beloved friend, Wendy, I wish you were here to share this with me.

For all surviving siblings, thank you for sharing your stories and your siblings with us, whether through groups, your beautiful memoirs, books, podcasts, and educational materials about sibling grief. I am unable to list you all, but you know who you are, and you have provided great comfort and support. This book is dedicated to you and your lost siblings. All of you are remembered and cherished.

I give my eternal thank you to all the generous donors and everyone who has championed and supported Celebration of Sisters for the past decade.

To my parents, Ellie and Benjamin (in blessed memory) Lipson, you provided me the strength and resilience to be who I am. The love you shared for sixty years, and the love and devotion for your daughters, shines through. Daddy, I am rolling with the punches.

To my spectacular daughters, Janie and Amy. I love you and you are forever the sunshine of my days. To my Brett and Matthew, I love you. And my grandson Benji, our new love and inspiration. As our beautiful family continues to grow, I hope you live out your dreams like your Nini has.

To my cherished sisters, Margie and Jane, I will always love you. This is for you. You are my anchors, my compass, my world, and you are forever beside me and in my heart.

Reading List

Throughout my journey, many resources provided comfort. *Adult Sibling Loss: Stories, Reflections and Ripples* by Brenda Marshall showed me, for the first time, that other adult siblings were out there feeling as I did. Other supports that helped immensely include the Compassionate Friends organization, and the Open to Hope Foundation. I hope these resources help you in your own grief journeys as much as they helped me.

Bonano, George. *The Other Side of Sadness: What the New Science of Bereavement Tells Us About Life After Loss.* New York: Basic Books, 2019.

Call, Colette M. "We Will Never Be Apart."

DeVita-Raeburn, Elizabeth. *The Empty Room: Surviving the Loss of a Brother or Sister at Any Age.* New York: Scribner, 2004.

Didion, Joan. *The Year of Magical Thinking.* New York: Vintage Books, 2007.

Gornick, Vivian. *Fierce Attachments.* New York: Farrar Straus Giroux, 1987.

Hainey, Michael. *After Visiting Friends: A Son's Story.* New York: Scribner, 2013.

Hallmark Cards, Inc. "Thinking of You Sister . . . and the Memories, Joy, and Love We Share." Kansas City, Missouri, 1978.

Handler, Jessica. *Invisible Sisters*. New York: PublicAffairs, 2009.

Hood, Ann. *Comfort: A Journey Through Grief.* New York: W.W. Norton & Co., 2008.

Marshall, Brenda. *Adult Sibling Loss: Stories, Reflections, and Ripples.* New York: Baywood Publishing, Inc., 2013.

Open to Hope. www.opentohope.com.

Sankovitch, Nina. *Tolstoy and the Purple Chair: My Year of Magical Reading.* New York: Harper Collins, 2011.

Sprague, Zander. *Making Lemonade: Choosing a Positive Pathway after Losing Your Sibling.* San Francisco: Paradiso Press, 2008.

Strauss, Darin. *Half a Life.* San Francisco: McSweeney's, 2010.

The Compassionate Friends. www.compassionatefriends.org.

We Love Memoirs. www.facebook.com/groups. welovememoirs/.

White, Dr. P. Gill. *Sibling Grief: Healing After the Death of a Sister or Brother.* Indiana: iUniverse, 2006.

Wolfelt, Alan D. *Healing the Adult Siblings Grieving Heart: 100 Practical Ideas After Your Brother or Sister Dies.* Colorado: Companion Press, 2008.

Wray, T. J. *Surviving the Death of a Sibling: Living Through Grief When an Adult Brother or Sister Dies.* New York: Three Rivers Press, 2003.

Celebration of Sisters
Skating Performances

Song Title / Sung by	Year of Judy's Performance
"I Will Always Love You" Whitney Houston	2012
"Through the Eyes of Love" Melissa Manchester	2013
"Flashdance . . . What a Feeling" Irene Cara	2014
"We Will Never Be Apart" J. Michael Call, Colette Call Lofgren	2015
"Downtown" Petula Clark	2015
"I've Gotta Be Me" Billy Porter	2016
"Beautiful" Carole King	2016 / 2019
"Both Sides Now" Judy Collins	2017 / 2018

Postponed due to COVID-19   2020

"Edelweiss"   2021
Andre Rieu

About the Author

Judy Lipson is the Founder and Chair of Celebration of Sisters, an annual ice skating fundraiser established in 2011 to commemorate the lives and memories of her beloved sisters to benefit Massachusetts General Hospital. Judy has published articles, given speeches, and been interviewed by the Open to Hope Organization, the Centering Organization, SKATING magazine, and in literature published by Massachusetts General Hospital, where she has maintained a close philanthropic relationship for more than twenty years.

Her passion for figure skating secured her the United States Figure Skating Association 2020 Get Up Champion Award.